EXPLORING
MILWAUKEE
WITH KIDS

WRITTEN BY CALIE HERBST
PRESENTED BY MKEWITHKIDS.COM

milwaukee
WITH KIDS

Exploring Milwaukee with Kids
By Calie Herbst / Presented by mkewithkids.com
ISBN: 978-1-948365-87-1
Library of Congress Control Number: 2018960335
Copyrighted © 2018 Calie Herbst, Founder of Milwaukee with Kids

First Edition
Cover design and interior layout and design by Samantha Williams

All Rights Reserved. Written permission must be secured from the publisher
to use or reproduce any part of this book, except for brief quotations in
critical reviews or articles.

For information, or for bulk orders, please contact:

Orange Hat Publishing
www.orangehatpublishing.com
Waukesha, WI

For Hudson, Rosie, and Mae.
May your lives be an extraordinary adventure.

ABOUT THE AUTHOR

In 2013, Calie Herbst, a former Spanish
teacher with three little ones, was frustrated
with how much time she spent searching
(too many) websites to find ways to make
the most of her time with her family. So she
founded Millwaukee With Kids. Her goal was
to find the best this city has to offer families
and share it with other parents. In one place.
You can hear Calie on B93.3 FM every Friday
and WTMJ Wisconsin Morning News on
Tuesday mornings. She's also been featured
on Fox 6's "Real Milwaukee" and "Studio A,"
and TMJ4's "Wisconsin Tonight."

IT TAKES A VILLAGE

While every attempt has been made to ensure that the information in this book is accurate at the time of publication, some information changes over time. It is recommended that you check a business's website for the most updated and accurate information about prices, hours, and more. Neither the author nor Milwaukee With Kids is responsible for any legal, medical, financial, or other hardships caused by acting on the information provided in this book. If you see something that should be changed or updated, please email hello@ mkewithkids.com and it may be changed in a future edition.

CONTENTS

INTRODUCTION

The message of this book is simple:

Family-friendly fun is all over Milwaukee.

Before I had kids, I loved to travel the world. In my twenties, I backpacked through Europe, Latin America, and beyond.

But now I'm a mom to three young children. Traveling often is just not as feasible as it once was, and I had to find a new way to satisfy my thirst for adventure.

So I started to search for the best that Milwaukee has to offer for kids and families. I combed through websites and scoped out parks and playgrounds. I visited nature centers and wandered through museums. I researched day trips and explored the arts scene. I roller skated and mini-golfed and apple-picked my way through southeastern Wisconsin.

And then I wrote this book to make it easy for other parents to do the same.

This handy guide will help you take advantage of all that this great city (and the surrounding area) has to offer. It will help you create lasting memories, discover new places, and experience new adventures with your family - without the price tag that comes with traveling the globe.

Parenting is both incredibly joyous and extremely challenging. My sincerest hope is that this book amplifies the joyous parts for you and your children, and makes life a little more fun.

Happy exploring!

-Calie Herbst

BOOK SYMBOLS

To help you determine the relative cost of activities throughout the book, I've used the following symbols:

(*) = free
($) = under ten dollars per person
($$) = ten to 20 dollars per person
($$$) = over 20 dollars per person

A cupcake symbol 🧁 indicates that the location offers birthday parties.

A campfire symbol 🔥 indicates that the location offers summer camp options.

Summer

Beach Days on Lake Michigan

Did you know that there are nine public beaches along the shores of beautiful Lake Michigan? Here they are listed from north to south, along with what you'll find at each one.

Doctors Park (*)
1870 E. Fox Ln.,
Fox Point, WI 53217
doctorsparkfriends.org
Located north of downtown Milwaukee in Fox Point, Doctors Park boasts nearly 50 acres of natural beauty on a bluff overlooking the lake. Near the parking lot, you'll find a playground and practice fields. From there, you can take a paved trail, stairs, or a dirt trail down to the beach. It's the perfect length nature hike for any child 4 and up, or a baby in a carrier.

Fun Fact: Doctors Park is located on the "point" from which Fox Point gets its name.

Klode Park (*)
5900 N. Lake Dr.,
Whitefish Bay, WI 53217
wfbvillage.org
Located north of downtown Milwaukee in Whitefish Bay, Klode Park offers breathtaking views of Lake Michigan, a winding path down to the rocky beach, open fields for running and sports, and a nice-sized playground for the kids.
Helpful hint: There's a clean, well-kept indoor bathroom in the shelter next to the playground.

Big Bay Park (*)
5000 N. Palisades Rd.,
Whitefish Bay, WI 53217
wfbvillage.org
Big Bay Park is a small and quiet oasis, tucked away in Whitefish Bay. You can enjoy a scenic overlook of the water, or walk down to the beach.

Atwater Beach (*)
East Capitol and North Lake Drive, Shorewood, WI 53211
villageofshorewood.org
When you first arrive, you'll see a playground in the park overlooking the lake. When you're ready to head down to the beach, you can get there via an impressively steep set of stairs, or a more gentle winding path. Once there, you'll find 800 feet of flat open beach. You'll be steps away from the city and shops on Capitol Drive, but the wild foliage of the tall bluff behind you will make you feel far from the city streets.

The park is also home to local family-friendly events throughout the summer, including July 4th fireworks, a Memorial Day celebration, and the annual Shorewood Men's Club Chicken Barbecue.

Don't miss it! Look for an impressive sculpture by Spanish artist Jaume Plensa of a contemplative man overlooking the beach. The sculpture was the center of controversy when passersby believed they saw anti-semitic messages in what was supposed to be random letters that make up the statue. The sculpture was later reinstalled without the controversial lettering.

Bradford Beach (*)
2400 N. Lincoln Memorial Dr., Milwaukee, WI 53211
bradfordbeachmke.com
A favorite of college students, Bradford Beach is bustling and boisterous. You can watch sand volleyball on any of the 35 courts, grab some shade in a tiki hut, or rent a cabana. Fried food and custard is available at the North Point Snack Shack, owned by Bartolotta, an award-winning local restaurant company. There's also a boat house building with convenient restrooms and a concession stand.

McKinley Beach (*)
1750 N. Lincoln Memorial Dr., Milwaukee, WI 53202
county.milwaukee.gov
Grab a fruit smoothie and iced coffee from local cafe Colectivo on the Lake and head north to the bay-shaped McKinley Beach. It's less crowded than neighboring Bradford Beach and has a playground to wear out your little ones. You can also catch beautiful views of the boats in McKinley Marina. If you're up for a walk, check out Veterans Park, just south of McKinley Beach. There's lots of space to run, fly a kite, or enjoy the lagoon.

South Shore Beach (*)

2900 S. Superior St.,
Milwaukee, WI 53207
county.milwaukee.gov

On the shores of Milwaukee's funky Bay View neighborhood, this beach offers picturesque views of South Shore Yacht Club and the downtown skyline. There's a large playground and a park with picnic tables and a sand volleyball court. In the summer, you can walk to South Shore Terrace, one of Milwaukee's newest beer gardens. However, this beach frequently closes due to bacteria levels. The Milwaukee County Parks system has implemented a green infrastructure project to improve the conditions.

Grant Park Beach (*)

100 S. Hawthorne Ave.,
South Milwaukee, WI 53172
county.milwaukee.gov

"Enter this wild wood and view the haunts of nature."

This message, written on a sign atop a covered bridge, welcomes you to the Seven Bridges Trail in Grant Park.

So it's no wonder that there are rumors the trail is haunted. But if you head there during the day, there's nothing spooky about it. The trail runs along a babbling creek, and leads all the way down to Lake Michigan, where you'll find a beautiful beach, a clean playground, and a beachside grill serving food and alcohol. The Sprecher & Milwaukee County Parks traveling beer garden typically stops by this park. You can also get a fish fry during the summer in the clubhouse.

To get there, enter Grant Park at South Lake Drive and Park Avenue, and travel about 1/8 mile. On your left you will find parking spaces with a path leading to the trail's main entrance.

Bender Park Beach (*)

4503 E. Ryan Rd.,
Oak Creek, WI 53154
county.milwaukee.gov

Bender Park is one of the county's newest parks, and it feels that way. It is well-maintained, not too crowded, and spacious. It has a harbor and large boat launches, but the dramatic bluffs overlooking Lake Michigan are what steal the show.

milwaukee
WITH KIDS

Swimming Ponds/Lakes

Brown Deer Pond ($)
4920 W. Green Brook Dr.,
Brown Deer, WI 53223
(414) 371-3070
browndeerwi.org
Head to Village Park in Brown Deer to swim in Brown Deer Pond, a one acre, chlorinated swimming facility with a sand beach. There is a large shallow water area for young kids, but be aware that inflatables and water wings are not allowed.

Fox Brook Park ($)
2925 N. Barker Rd.,
Brookfield, WI 53045
(262) 548-7801
waukeshacounty.gov
If you're looking for a slice of classic Americana, head to Fox Brook Park on a summer afternoon. The man-made lake has a sandy bottom and clean, warm water to swim in. The lifeguards will help keep your little ones safe, and there is a well-maintained bathroom nearby. Be forewarned, there is no designated place to rinse off. *Helpful hint: Take a hike around the mile-long paved trail that winds around the lake. You'll discover three wildlife viewing areas!*

Lakefront Park (*)
222 W. Wisconsin Ave.,
Pewaukee, WI 53072
(262) 691-0770
cityofpewaukee.us
Lakefront Park *(above)* seems to emerge out of a Norman Rockwell painting with it's small town charm and quaint shops along the shores of Pewaukee Lake. Spend your days relaxing in the park or swimming in the lake. Enjoy the warm summer evenings strolling down Main Street.
Pro tip: On Wednesdays in the summer, enjoy free live music at Waterfront Wednesday. Or catch one of the free, action-packed waterski shows on Thursday evenings between Memorial Day and Labor Day.

Menomonee Park ($)
W220 N7884 Town Line Rd.,
Menomonee Falls, WI 53051
(262) 548-7801
waukeshacounty.gov
Nestled in Menomonee Park is the 16-acre Menomonee Quarry Lake, formerly known as Lannon Quarry. The water is clean and clear, and lifeguards are on duty during swimming hours. There is a swimming area for toddlers and small children. It's a lovely place to go hiking, fishing, or camping.

14

Minooka Park ($)
1927 E. Sunset Dr.,
Waukesha, WI 53186
(262) 548-7801
waukeshacounty.gov
The largest park in the Waukesha County Parks System offers plenty of family-friendly hiking over hundreds of acres, and you can cool off in the swimming beach and pond. You can even bring your pets along to visit the fenced-in dog park.

Mukwonago Park ($)
W325, S9945 County Hwy LO,
Mukwonago, WI 53149
(262) 548-7801
waukeshacounty.gov
About 30 minutes north of Milwaukee, you'll find Mukwonago Park. This park is typically less crowded and, for a small car fee, you'll enjoy a swimming pond, hiking trails, a dog park, and campgrounds. There are changing rooms, bathrooms, and a shower at the pond.

Muskego Park ($)
S83W20370 Janesville Rd.,
Muskego, WI 53150
(262) 679-0310
waukeshacounty.gov
Hike through the hardwood forests of this peaceful 153 acre park, and swim in a small pond with a swimming beach.

Naga-Waukee Park ($)
651 Hwy 83,
Hartland, WI 53029
(262) 548-7801
waukeshacounty.gov
Naga-Waukee Park offers swimming in pretty Lake Nagawicka along with a playground nearby, plenty of camping grounds, and a chance to spot wildlife in their natural habitat. Take a peaceful moment to walk along the boardwalk that runs through the trees and along the lake.

Water Parks & Pools

Jefferson County

Watertown Aquatic Center in Riverside Park ($)
1009 Perry St.,
Watertown, WI 53094
(920) 262-8085
ci.watertown.wi.us
If you're up for the 45 minute drive from Milwaukee, this heated municipal pool features a large zero depth area, a 12 foot mushroom waterfall, floor fountains, and waterslides for the little ones. If you dare, you can take a thrilling ride down the 216 foot waterslide or plunge down the 24 foot dropslide. There is also a one-meter diving board and a 25 meter lap lane. When you're done swimming, you can spend time in the sandy playground area, play volleyball, or chow down at the concession stand and eating areas. The bathhouse offers coin-operated lockers.

Milwaukee County

Top pick: TOSA Pool at Hoyt Park ($) 🧁
1800 N. Swan Blvd.,
Wauwatosa, WI 53226
(414) 302-9160
friendsofhoytpark.org
Close to the city and packed with fun, TOSA Pool is the perfect place to spend a hot summer afternoon with the whole family. It is an award-winning public pool that offers a large, colorful play structure, water slides, in-pool umbrellas that provide shade, and swimming classes for kids and adults. You don't have to be a member to swim, but there are fun members-only events throughout the summer.

Cool Waters Family Aquatic Park ($) 🧁
2028 S. 124th St.,
West Allis, WI 53227
(414) 257-8098
county.milwaukee.gov
Cool Waters has a heated pool with a giant tube and body water slides, water slides for young children, interactive water toys, a playground, sand volleyball courts, and a cafe.

David F. Schulz Aquatic Center in Lincoln Park ($) 🧁
1301 W. Hampton Ave.,
Milwaukee, WI 53209
(414) 257-8098
county.milwaukee.gov
Race down the tube and body waterslides, float along in the lazy river, or swim in the heated pool. There are spray jets, water troughs, and a bucket dump for the kids, plus a concession stand once everyone gets hungry.

Hales Corners Pool ($) 🧁
5765 S. New Berlin Rd.,
Hales Corners, WI 53130
(414) 529-3622
halescornerspark.com
This well-kept park and pool is supported by a dedicated community group. Dive into the 50 yard deep water pool, or head to the pool house where you'll find concessions, a pool table and foosball table, video games, cable, and wi-fi.

Besides the pool, Hales Corners Park boasts tennis and basketball courts, a climbing rock, playground, wading pools for young kids, walking path, and two baseball fields.

Pelican Cove Family Water Park ($) 🧁
Kosciuszko Park
2201 S. 7th St.,
Milwaukee, WI 53215
(414) 257-8098
county.milwaukee.gov
At Pelican Cove, you'll find huge waterslides for big kids and smaller waterslides for young kids. There are also spraying and splashing interactive water toys for kids of all ages.

16

Sheridan Pool in Sheridan Park ($) 🧁

4800 S. Lake Dr.,
Cudahy, WI 53110
(414) 481-4731
county.milwaukee.gov

This park is located on Lake Michigan, and there is a trail that will take you right down to the water. The views of downtown Milwaukee can't be beat. Cool off at the pool, complete with a drop slide and water mushrooms.
Helpful Hint: Sheridan Park is a great place to watch the fireworks on the fourth of July and watch planes taking off and landing.

More Pools

Fox Point Pool ($) 🧁

7100 N. Santa Monica Blvd.,
Fox Point, WI 53217
414-351-8908
vil.fox-point.wi.us

Grobschmidt Pool ($) 🧁

2500 15th Ave.,
South Milwaukee, WI 53172
(414) 762-4919
county.milwaukee.gov

Holler Pool ($) 🧁

5151 S. 6th St.,
Milwaukee, WI 53221
(414) 481-7160
county.milwaukee.gov

Jackson Pool ($) 🧁

3500 W. Forest Home Ave.,
Milwaukee, WI 53215
(414) 384-2028
county.milwaukee.gov

McCarty Pool ($) 🧁

2567 S. 79th St.,
West Allis, WI 53219
(414) 327-2519
county.milwaukee.gov

Washington Park Pool ($) 🧁

1859 N. 40th St.,
Milwaukee, WI 53208
(414) 344-5400
county.milwaukee.gov

Wilson Pool ($) 🧁

4001 S. 20th St.,
Milwaukee, WI 53221
(414) 281-4498
county.milwaukee.gov

Ozaukee County

Cedarburg Community Pool ($) 🧁

W67 N851 Evergreen Blvd.,
Cedarburg, WI 53012
(262) 375-7665
ci.cedarburg.wi.us

Located in Cedarburg's Centennial Park, this community pool offers a snake slide for young kids or a faster slide for older kids. There are diving boards and a human foosball court, too. Grab a bite to eat at the snack bar and get sandy in the kids play area.

Mequon Community Pool ($)

11335 N. Cedarburg Rd.,
Mequon, WI 53092
(262) 242-9923
ci.mequon.wi.us

Take a relaxing dip in the shallow end or jump off the diving boards in the deep end. There is a separate zero-depth wading area for babies and toddlers. Certified lifeguards staff the pool at all times. Check their website for "dive-in" movie night dates and times.

Pirates Hollow Waterpark ($) 🧁

201 N. Webster St.,
Port Washington, WI 53074
(262) 284-7679
portwashington.recdesk.com

The water slide here is a drop slide, and there are also diving boards and water mushrooms. There is a zero-depth entry side for young children.

Washington County

Veteran's Memorial Aquatic Center ($) 🧁

777 S. Main St.,
Hartford, WI 53027
(262) 670-3730
ci.hartford.wi.us

Located about 45 minutes from the city, this new family water park opened in 2016 and offers something for everyone. You'll find an eight-lane, 50 meter pool leading into a fan-shaped zero-depth swimming area. Go it alone down the bright green open flume waterslide with plunge pool, or grab a buddy for the purple two-person raft slide. Relax in the Lazy River circling the water area. You can also dive off two diving boards, or explore the toddler area with a small fish-shaped slide.

You'll be required to shower before entering in the clean and well-maintained locker rooms. The safe, family atmosphere is enforced by the lifeguards. There are no shoes or sandals, and no running on the deck. A concession stand nearby serves typical fast foods, and there's plenty of shaded area to lounge around without getting burned.

Waukesha County

Buchner Pool ($) 🧁

223 Oakland Ave., Waukesha, WI 53186
(262) 524 3726
waukesha-wi.gov

Dubbed "Waukesha's Classic Swimming Pool," you'll find an Olympic size pool with a lap lane always open, a separate wading pool for young kids, a one meter diving board and two meter slide, plus basketball and volleyball courts. The staff is comprised of Red Cross-certified lifeguards and instructors.

Elm Grove Swimming Pool ($) 🧁

Village Park, 13600 Juneau Blvd., Elm Grove, WI 53122
(262) 782-6940
elmgrovewi.org

Keep an eye out for special family swim times at this friendly community pool.

Horeb Springs Aquatic Center ($) 🏠

330 Spring St.,
Waukesha, WI 53188
(262) 524-3727
waukesha-wi.gov
This zero-depth entry pool has water that's relatively warm, two flume slides, sprinklers and a high diving board. You'll appreciate the clean dressing rooms and full concession area.

Wiberg Aquatic Center ($) 🏠

Wirth Park
2585 N. Pilgrim Rd.,
Brookfield, WI 53005
(262) 787-3901
cityofbrookfield.com
Brookfield's community pool is 50 meters, with a water slide, two diving boards, a sand play area, geysers, a playground, and more. There is a concession stand and plenty of shade.

Splash Pads & Wading Pools

Hart Park Playground and Splash Pad (*)

7201 W. State St.,
Wauwatosa, WI 53213
(414) 471-8420
wauwatosa.net
The Splash Pad in Hart Park is adjacent to a natural themed, all access playground with log balance beams, climbing ropes, and an eagle's nest. There is a park pavilion nearby for bathroom breaks and changing. You can also make an afternoon of it by exploring the surrounding park and perusing the charming downtown Wauwatosa area nearby.

Hickory Park Splash Pad (*)

N165 W20330 Hickory Ln.,
Jackson, WI 53037
(262) 677-9665
jacksonparkrec.recdesk.com
This fenced-in Splash Pad is located just outside the Jackson Community Center. It is open to the public every day from Memorial Day to Labor Day, 10:00 a.m. until 7:00 p.m.

Kinderberg Park Sprayground (*)

N106W15060 Buckthorn Dr., Germantown, WI 53022
(262) 250-4710
village.germantown.wi.us
The colorful sprayground is located in Kinderberg Park, and it's open daily from 10:00 a.m. to 8:00 p.m. Memorial Day through Labor Day.

Lake Country Rotary Splash Pad in Nixon Park (*)

175 E. Park Ave,
Hartland, WI 53029
lakecountryrotarysplashpad.
com

Located in Nixon Park, the Splash Pad is free to kids of all ages and is open from 10:00 a.m. until 7:00 p.m. daily.

Milwaukee County Parks Splash Pads (*)

For the most up-to-date list of splash pads and wading pools throughout the Milwaukee County Parks, go to countyparks.com.

Splash pads:
Carver, 911 W. Brown St., Milwaukee, WI 53205
Clarke Square, 2330 W. Vieau Pl., Milwaukee, WI 53204
Dineen, 6901 W. Vienna Ave., Milwaukee, WI 53216
Gordon, 1321 E. Locust St., Milwaukee, WI 53212
Lindbergh, 3629 N. 16th St., Milwaukee, WI 53206
Madison, 9800 W. Glendale Ave., Wauwatosa, WI 53225
Moody, 2201 W. Auer Ave., Milwaukee, WI 53206

Wading pools:
Columbus, 7301 W. Courtland Ave., Milwaukee, WI 53218
Cooper, 8701 W. Chambers St., Milwaukee, WI 53222
Hales Corners, 5765 S. New Berlin Rd., Hales Corners, WI 53130
Jacobus, 6501 Hillside Ln., Wauwatosa, WI 53213

Rainbow, 700 S. 119th St., West Allis, WI 53214
Smith, 5462 N. 33rd St., Milwaukee, WI 53209
Tiefenthaler, 2501 W. Galena St., Milwaukee, WI 53205
Walker Square, 1031 S. 9th St., Milwaukee, WI 53204
West Milwaukee, 5000 W. Burnham St., West Milwaukee, WI 53219

Oak Creek Splash Pad (*)

361 W. Town Square Way, Oak Creek, WI 53154

This splash pad is part of the Drexel Town Square shopping center which boasts a new City Hall, Library, and lots of retail shops and restaurants. This community space is open with pedestrian-friendly walkways. (Be forewarned - public restrooms are hard to find.)

Boating

Milwaukee Kayak Company ($$$)

318 S. Water St.,
Milwaukee, WI 53204
(414) 301-2240
milwaukeekayak.com

You can easily coast along the Milwaukee River with your child (11 and under) by renting a tandem kayak or canoe with the Milwaukee Kayak Company, located in the Harbor District across from the Third Ward. All the boat rentals come with a paddle and life jackets.

Milwaukee Community Sailing Center ($$$)

1450 N. Lincoln Drive,
Milwaukee, WI 53202
(414) 277-9094
sailingcenter.org

Located in Milwaukee's Veteran Park, the sailing center offers classes for kids starting at age eight. The "Prams in the Park" program for kids ages eight to twelve introduces sailing in the Discovery World lagoon. Students learn water safety, rigging, sail theory, basic maneuvers, and capsize recovery drills. Scholarships are available, and membership is not required to take the classes.

Milwaukee Yacht Club ($$$)

1700 N. Lincoln Memorial Drive, Milwaukee, WI 53202
(414) 271-4455
milwaukeeyc.com

The Milwaukee Yacht Club is the oldest of its kind on Lake Michigan, located near McKinley Marina. They offer sailing classes to kids as young as six years old. Classes are open to the public, but they are small.

S/V Denis Sullivan Family Sails ($$$)

Discovery World
500 N. Harbor Dr.,
Milwaukee, WI 53202
(414) 765-9966
discoveryworld.org

What is the S/V Denis Sullivan?
This unique vessel is a re-creation of a three-masted, Great Lakes schooner from the 1800's and it's the only one in the world of its kind. During the warm months it travels around the Great Lakes and Canada hosting groups of all ages to educate them about maritime history and the ecological health of the Great Lakes.

What can you do on a Family Sail?
During the two hour Family Sail, families can take part in raising the sails, chat with the crew about the ship and their jobs, take in stunning views of Milwaukee, and enjoy a complimentary snack and beverage. Kids are also invited to dress up as their favorite pirate or superhero.

Families are encouraged to roam around the ship during the sail. Explore the warm, earthy colors and textures of the 19th century and the enormous steering wheel, small gift shop, and large silver bell that commemorates the construction date. The interesting nooks and crannies seem to never end.

The ship is run by a friendly crew of passionate sailors who love to chat about what they do. You can help them hoist up the sails onto the 95 foot tall mast and practice techniques for laying lines and tying knots. You'll learn about maritime culture, its clever commands, and the irreverent fun and freedom of being a sailor.

How old do you have to be?
Kids of all ages will enjoy the sail, but especially kids four and older. This is a truly unique experience for the whole family.

Pro Tip: If you're on a tight budget, you can explore the ship during the month of October when it transforms into a "Haunted Tall Ship." Find out more in the Halloween section of this book.

Pewaukee Lake Sailing School at Pewaukee Yacht Club ($$$)
N22W28204 Edgewater Dr., Pewaukee, WI 53702
(262) 691-9927
plss.org
The Pewaukee Lake Sailing School offers a wide variety of sailing classes starting as early as age five. In the introductory class, kids learn important water safety lessons and the basics of sailing. Classes for school-aged kids and teenagers are offered, as well.

Beer Gardens

(Yes, they're family friendly!)

By definition, a biergarten is simply an open-air space where beer and food are served. But in reality, they are so much more than that. Popular in Bavaria and Germany, beer gardens are a festive place for people to get together and delight in good food, beer, and the outdoors. Many have popped up over the years around Milwaukee, and they are definitely family-friendly.

Top pick:
Estabrook Beer Garden
Estabrook Park
4600 Estabrook Dr.,
Milwaukee, WI 53217
(414) 226-2728
estabrookbeergarden.com
Estabrook Beer Garden is located on a bluff in Estabrook Park, just steps from a playground and above a waterfall on the banks of the Milwaukee River. Whether you arrive by foot, bike, car, kayak, or canoe, it's the perfect place to spend the afternoon with your kids. The park is packed with nature trails and boasts a disc golf course, dog park, soccer fields, and a riverfront boardwalk. The beer garden features imported beer served in a heavy glass mug, and food includes bratwurst, hot dogs and the Famous Giant Fresh Baked Pretzel. You can bring your own favorite beer stein, and your own food and soft drinks as well. Enjoy live music and a very family-friendly atmosphere.

Hubbard Park
Beer Garden
3565 N. Morris Blvd.,
Shorewood, WI 53211
(414) 332-4207
hubbardparkbeergarden.com
Hubbard Park Beer Garden is a traditional Old World Beer Garden located along the Oak Leaf Trail bike path in peaceful Hubbard Park just south of Capitol Drive. You can try local beers, non-alcoholic drinks, and a selection of food. Parking is limited so biking and walking is encouraged.

Humboldt Park Beer Garden

3000 S. Howell Ave.,
Milwaukee, WI 53207
(414) 418-2864
milwaukeescraftbeergarden.com

The Humboldt Park Beer Garden, the product of a partnership between Milwaukee County Parks and St. Francis Brewing Company, serves craft soda, beer, wine, and food. It is located just outside of the Humboldt Park pavilion and close to the playground. It also has indoor seating.

Pro tip: While you're there, take a stroll around the nearby lagoon and enjoy the enormous trees, wildlife, and historic terrace in the park. You may even spot a tiny fairy house at the base of some of the larger trees.

The Landing

Hoyt Park (1800 N. Swan Blvd, Wauwatosa, WI 53226)
(414) 302-9160
friendsofhoytpark.org

Share a table with friendly strangers at The Landing at Hoyt Park and take in live music, draft beer, wine, Cranky Al's pizza, and Bavarian-style pretzels and brats.

Sprecher Brewing Outdoor Oasis

Richard E. Maslowski Community Park
2200 W. Bender Rd.,
Glendale, WI 53209
glendale-wi.org

Enjoy craft beer and soda for the kids at this beer garden, located next to a brand new amphitheater and handicap accessible playground.

Third Space Brewing Beer Garden

1505 W. St. Paul Ave.,
Milwaukee WI 53233
(414) 909-2337
thirdspacebrewing.com

This award-winning brewery is a relative newcomer on the Milwaukee beer scene, but it has taken it by storm. Their urban beer garden, adjacent to the tap room, is dog friendly, kid friendly, and always packed with fun. Outside and carry-in food is welcome. They often host special events and bring in food trucks, so check their website for updates.

Sprecher Traveling Beer Garden

Parks around the city
county.milwaukee.gov

For the past few years, the Milwaukee County Parks Traveling Beer Garden has toured throughout the parks of Milwaukee County thanks to a partnership with Sprecher Brewing Company. Each of the stops feature craft beer, gourmet sodas, and other refreshments and food.

Insider tip: Look for the Sprecher converted vintage fire truck that now serves as a 12 tap fire truck.

Berry and Cherry Picking

Picking fresh berries on a local farm is a unique way to spend an afternoon with your children, and helps them learn where their food comes from in a hands-on way.

Quick reference:

Strawberries: Mid-late June
Sugar Snap Peas: June
Cherries: Early July
Raspberries: Mid-July
Blackberries: Late July -
Early August

*Always, always, always be sure to call ahead for hours and the latest information. Picking times and dates depend on weather and availability, and it's always changing.

Top pick: Walvoord's Berry Farm ($$)

W2160 Smies Rd.,
Oostburg, WI 53070
(920) 668-6481
walvoordsberryfarm.tripod.com
This berry farm has small-town charm, friendly staff, and sweet pick-your-own strawberries. You can also pick-your-own sweet podded peas. The crops are well maintained, and your kids will love the tractor ride out to the fields.

Top pick: Steffen's Cherry Orchard ($$)

N633 McIntyre Rd.,
Fort Atkinson, WI 53538
(920) 563-9608
steffenscherryorchard.com
If you love cherries and are up for a bit of a drive, head to this family-owned and operated orchard during cherry-picking season. The season typically starts in early July, and it doesn't last long. Stroll through picturesque, flowering cherry trees, and take advantage of their mechanical pitter.

Basse's Taste of Country Farm Market ($$) 🧁

3190 County Line Rd.,
Colgate WI 53017
(262) 628-2626
bassesfarms.com

Enjoy a breezy tractor ride out to the field and pick from 120,000 strawberry plants. They also offer you-pick raspberries, and they are one of the only places where you can pick-your-own blackberries. The picking system is very organized, and their staff will assign you to a row. In the country store you can purchase pre-picked strawberries, peas, and rhubarb, and choose from homemade strawberry donuts, pies, pound cake, breads and strawberry sundaes.

Apple Barn Orchard and Winery ($$) 🧁

W6384 Sugar Creek Rd.,
Elkhorn, WI 53121
(262) 728-3266
applebarnorchardandwinery.com
Here you can mix strawberry picking and wine tasting. What could be better? But don't be confused - Apple Barn Orchard and Winery is located on Sugar Creek Road with one of the cross streets being Sugar Creek Street.

Barthel Fruit Farm ($$)

12246 N. Farmdale Rd 99W,
Mequon, WI 53097
(262) 242-2737
barthelfruitfarm.com
People love Barthel Fruit Farm for its well-organized picking system, convenient location, and friendly staff. They tend 15 acres of strawberries, and you can pick-your-own strawberries and sugar snap peas during the summer.

Brehmer's U-Pick Pumpkins & Strawberries ($$)

5805 Clover Rd.,
Hartford, WI 53027
(262) 673-6527
Brehmer's offers pick-your-own strawberries and they do not use pesticides on their plants. Bonus: the rows are wide enough for strollers and wheelchairs.

Polzin Farms ($$)
1758 Hwy I,
Grafton, WI 53024
(262) 375-3276

Pick-your-own strawberries,
sugar snap peas & sweet corn.

Thompson Strawberry Farm ($$)
14000 75th St.,
Bristol, WI 53104
(262) 857-2353
thompsonstrawberryfarm.com
Pick-your-own strawberries
and raspberries.

Kid-friendly Summer Festivals

Top pick: Festa Italiana ($$)
July
Henry Maier Festival Park
639 E. Summerfest Pl.,
Milwaukee, WI 53202
(414) 223-2808
festaitaliana.com
For the littlest bambinos, Festa
Italiana offers a Children's Stage
with kid-friendly performances
and activities, a free Kidzone
with inflatables, plus bocce ball,
gondola rides, and a kids' pizza
making contest. You'll also see
the sky light up with Bartolotta
fireworks every night.

Get in free: Children under 12 are
admitted free during the entire
festival, and they typically offer
free admission for all on Sunday.

Top pick: Strawberry Fest (*)

Late June
Downtown Cedarburg - Washington Ave.
Cedarburg, WI 53012
(888) 894-4001
cedarburgfestival.org

If you can handle the crowds, you'll find tons for the kids to do at Cedarburg's free annual Strawberry Fest, and you'll get to enjoy some tasty summer treats while you're there. You can try the original strawberry brat, or some sweet strawberry shortcake, among seemingly endless options. Stroll down the street and explore the white-topped booths, or head over to Cedar Creek Park where the bulk of the kids' activities take place. You'll typically find kid-friendly live entertainment, a duck race, a petting zoo, lots of games, and prizes.

Top pick: Irish Fest ($$)

August
Henry Maier Festival Park
639 E. Summerfest Pl.,
Milwaukee, WI 53202
(414) 476-3378
irishfest.com

Did you know that Milwaukee Irish Fest is the largest celebration of its kind, anywhere in the world? The sights, sounds, and tastes of Ireland come alive each year along the lakefront, and there are tons of unique activities for kids of all ages.

Pick up a Pirate Paddy Passport and collect stamps throughout the grounds. You'll be rewarded with kid-friendly activities and prizes at each stop. En route, you may catch a parade packed with Celtic Canines, pipe and drum units, vikings, and more.

One of the most beloved areas at Irish Fest is the Leprechaun Village, where families can explore tiny structures including a workshop, pub, performance stage, and bank vault.

Just beyond the giant rainbow, check out the Children's Area with Lili-Putt mini golf, crafts, Highland games, and prizes at the Pot O' Gold. Explore the Children's Cultural Area on the playground, including a Children's Tea Room, the Irish Discovery Zone, and interactive demonstrations.

The Celtic Canine area is another must-see, where you can meet and pet some of Ireland's most popular dog breeds, talk with the Midwest's top breeders, and learn about grooming, general care, and training. There's also a demonstration area highlighting obedience, agility, and hunting skills.

Traditional Irish fare includes bridies (turnovers), sausage rolls, shepherd's pie, bangers and mash, corned beef and cabbage, and a variety of stuffed baked potatoes. For a sweet dessert, try Bailey's cheesecake, shamrock cookies or Irish cream puffs.

Get in free: Children 12 and under always get in free, and the festival typically offers free admission on Sunday after attending mass or with a non-perishable food item.

Cuban Day Street Festival
May
facebook.com/cubanitas
Each year, local restaurant Cubanitas hosts the lively Cuban Day Street Festival. It includes live music, free dance instruction, kids activities, and delicious Cuban food for sale.

Locust Street Festival of Music & Art (*)
June
Locust Street between Humboldt and Holton
locuststreetfestival.com
Local music and art lovers will love the six outdoor music stages and dozens of artists and vendors featured at the Locust Street Festival. The festival also hosts a thunderous drum circle, children's activities, and food and drink vendors.

Polish Fest ($$)
June
Henry Maier Festival Park
639 E. Summerfest Pl.,
Milwaukee, WI 53202
polishfest.org
Besides reveling in the lively polka, colorful folk costumes, and traditional polish sausage, you can head to the children's stage that often features comedians, magicians, escape artists, dance shows, Kohl's Wild Theater, and more. Stop by the Cultural Village to see demonstrations of traditional Polish crafts such as wycinanki (paper cutting), pisanki (decorated eggs), and wianki (floral head wreaths). The Maly Sklep (little store) sells traditional Polish pottery and other folk art. There are even live sheepdogs.

Free admission for dads! Polish Fest is usually held over Father's Day week, and dads are typically offered free admission when accompanied by their child. Check their website for other admission deals.

Juneteenth Day Parade
June
2460 N. 6th St.,
Milwaukee, WI 53212
(414) 372-3770
juneteenthdaymilwaukee.com
Juneteenth Day is June 19th, and it commemorates the ending of slavery in the United States. Today, it is a celebration of African American achievement. The celebration in Milwaukee includes a lively parade, a Miss Juneteenth Day Pageant, and food vendors.

Greek Fest (*)
June
Wisconsin State Fair Park
640 S. 84th St.,
West Allis, WI 53214
annunciationwi.org
Be entertained by traditional Greek music and dancing, along with a Greek Market full of imported goods and artifacts. Taste fresh, authentic Greek food including gyros, Greek chicken, lamb, saganaki (fried cheese), souvlaki (skewers), baklava (sweet dessert made with phyllo dough) and loukoumades (fried dough). Games and rides for children of all ages are available. Admission is free, but you'll have to pay for parking.

Summer Soulstice (*)
June
2122 N. Prospect Ave.,
Milwaukee, WI 53202
(414) 272-5823
theeastside.org
The trendy East Side hosts Summer Soulstice, a free showcase of local bands, visual artists, Milwaukee makers, creation stations, East Side restaurants, dodgeball and BMX stunt bikes, and family-friendly crafts and activities.

Summerfest with kids ($$)
summerfest.com
Every year Milwaukeeans of all ages flock to the Henry Maier Festival Park for one of the longest running music festivals in the world - Summerfest. And although your memories of this cream city tradition may not be kid-friendly, the festival itself most certainly is. Here are some of the best things to do with kids:

The Elizabeth "Bo" Black Family Fountain: Hopping around in this iconic splash pad is the perfect way to keep cool on a hot summer day.

Did you know? Kosciuszko Park is named after Polish patriot Tadeusz Kosciuszko? He was an engineer and military mastermind in the 18th century and supported the American Revolution. In his will, he designated large funds to be used for freeing and educating African-American slaves. Polish Fest celebrates this national figure, and gives Milwaukee an opportunity to learn more about Polish culture.

Children's Theater & Playzone:
Visit the daily lineup pages for information on daily, family-focused performers and show times.

Kohl's Captivation Station:
This area lives up to its name, captivating children of all ages with hands on art projects, live theater and family friendly performers. Families can meet new characters and puppets and enjoy wildlife adventures and songs in conservation-themed performances by Kohl's Wild Theater, part of the Zoological Society of Milwaukee. You can also create a one-of-a-kind art project with Kohl's Color Wheels, an extension of the Milwaukee Art Museum. For innovative design projects, stop by the Kohl's Design it! Mobile Lab. You'll learn techniques and methods from design professionals from Discovery World.

Ferris Wheel: The Summerfest "Wheel in the Sky" on the north end of the grounds offers spectacular views of Summerfest, Milwaukee's downtown, and Lake Michigan. It operates from noon - 11:30 p.m. daily.

Skyglider: There's nothing like your first ride on the sky glider. The gentle ride offers a scenic view of Henry Maier Festival Park, Lake Michigan, and the entertainment below.

Get in free: To save on admission and take advantage of food and beverage deals, check the schedule for Kohl's Family Day and Children's Fest Day.

Helpful hints:
-Be aware of the Lost Children's Area near the Mid Gate for children who become separated from their parents. Children are brought to this secure area and checked in by a member of the Summerfest staff.

-Create an identification wristband for your child at any main gate.

-Nursing? No problem. Look for a Nursing Mothers Station in the Children's Area and at the South Gate Information Booth. These areas provide a comfortable, private and convenient space for nursing moms.

Fireworks Kite Festival (*)
Early July
Veterans Park
1010 N. Lincoln Memorial Dr., Milwaukee, WI 53202
(414) 273-5483
giftofwings.com
The Fireworks Kite Festival is a just-for-fun kite fly of which everyone is welcome to participate. A huge area of Veterans Park is set aside just for kite-fliers, and the kite-filled sky is an impressive sight to behold. Plus, it's the perfect way to get the best seat in the house to the fireworks show along the lakefront.

Bristol Renaissance Fair ($$$)

Saturdays, Sundays & Labor Day
July - early September
12550 120th Ave.,
Kenosha, WI 53142
(847) 395-7773
renfair.com

Climb a castle wall, shoot bow and arrows, and throw an axe all in one day. If you love all things medieval, you should definitely step back in time to attend this festival spread across 30 acres and 20 stages. Medieval characters in full dress make for an authentic renaissance experience. Families can watch fully armored jousts, parades, and entertainers in the streets all day long. You'll also find plenty of rides, games, arts and crafts, food, drink, and music. Plus, check their website for special KidQuests.

Bastille Days (*)

July
Cathedral Square Park
825 N. Jefferson St.,
Milwaukee, WI 53202
(414) 271-1416
eastown.com

Marked by the signature 43-foot Eiffel Tower replica and hourly light shows, Milwaukee hosts one of the nation's largest French-themed celebrations each July. The international marketplace comes alive with the sizzling sights and smells of French and Cajun cuisine.
Pro tip: Kids' and Family Day is usually Saturday, offering soccer and dance lessons, cooking demonstrations, and more.

Washington County Fair ($)

July
3000 Pleasant Valley Rd.,
West Bend, WI 53095
(262) 677-5060
wcfairpark.com

The Family Expo Center is the center of kid-friendly activities. Enjoy horse shows, the small animal tents, contests, 4-H performances, tractor pulls, and much more.

German Fest ($$)

July
Henry Maier Festival Park
639 E. Summerfest Pl.,
Milwaukee, WI 53202
germanfest.com

The sounds of carousel organs and the smell of German cuisine - sausage, sauerkraut, and schnitzel - float through the festival grounds, bringing German culture to life. Families head there each year for the Dachsund Derby and costume contest, the Glockenspiel clock that comes to life every few hours, traditional "tracht" clothing, German dance performances, mascots, and parades.
Get in free: Kids under 12 are always free. Sunday is typically free during specified times for those who bring non-perishable food items. Check the website for updated information.

32

Art and Chalk Fest at MOWA (*)

Museum of Wisconsin Art
205 Veterans Ave.,
West Bend, WI 53095
(262) 334-9638
wisconsinart.org
This free outdoor fine arts and crafts festival features artist booths as well as chalk artists, art activities for all ages, live entertainment and music, food vendors, a beer garden, and more.

Ozaukee County Fair (*)

W67N866 Washington Ave.,
Cedarburg, WI 53012
(262) 375-6185
ozaukeecountyfair.com
Held each year in Cedarburg, the Ozaukee County Fair is one of the last free county fairs in Wisconsin. You'll find games, rides, animals, fair food, truck pulls, demonstrations, and live music.

Milwaukee Journal Sentinel a la Carte ($$)

August
10001 W. Bluemound Rd.,
Milwaukee, WI 53226
(414) 771-3040
milwaukeezoo.org
Grab your lawn chairs and spend a relaxing summer evening at the Zoo. This annual event showcases the best flavors Milwaukee has to offer, plus top local and national bands performing throughout the grounds. Find your perfect grassy spot or picnic table, and try food from dozens of the area's best restaurants. Parents can enjoy a glass of wine and live music in the Giraffe Village Wine Tent. Kids will love the arts and crafts projects and special animal exhibits. Zoo rides are available for purchase.

Milwaukee Air & Water Show (*)

July
milwaukeeairshow.com
You won't be able to miss it! (Even if you want to.) Milwaukee's lakefront roars with impressive military aircrafts like the Blue Angels during the Air & Water Show, and it's free to watch from afar. You can also purchase tickets for front row center seats.

Brady Street Festival (*)

July
bradystreet.org
Head to funky Brady Street for live entertainment all day and night from local bands on four stages. Stunt bike and tumbling shows, arts and crafts, and a rock climbing wall make this a family-friendly event.

Mexican Fiesta ($$)

August
Summerfest Grounds
mexicanfiesta.org
Discover Mexican culture at Mexican Fiesta. You'll find upbeat mariachi music, vibrant folk costumes, and steaming tamales. You can browse authentic folk art for sale, and visit the impressive, colorful sanctuary honoring Our Lady of Guadalupe.

Milwaukee Dragon Boat Festival (*)

August
milwaukeedragonboatfest.org
Vibrant colored boats race across the water during this exciting festival put on by the Milwaukee Chinese Community Center. The event also showcases traditional Chinese folk music, dance, games, martial arts, and lantern making.

Wisconsin State Fair ($$)

August
wistatefair.org
Wisconsin State Fair is a celebration of agriculture and livestock, local delicacies, and fried food. The smell of corn on the cob (and manure) is in the air, and so is a sense of pride for all things Wisconsin. Every family seems to have small traditions in place around this event. If your family doesn't, or you'd like some fresh ideas for your annual trip, read on.

Of the many barns and animals to visit, a must-visit stop is the Discovery Barnyard, where you'll get to see cuddly baby animals of all kinds. There are also hands-on sensory tables for young kids and other child-friendly activities.

Outside of the wonderfully smelly animal barns, activities for kids are at every turn. The Kohl's Activity Zone is a free area with a number of white tented booths offering children's crafts, design projects, conservation-themed theater performances, and educational activities for kids.

Be on the lookout for strolling street entertainers who claim some serious talents from guessing your weight accurately to juggling fire. You might also catch a parade which take place daily and feature mascots, tractors, marching bands, and more.

It will be difficult to resist the big yellow slide, which has been around for over fifty years. Hop onto a burlap sack and take a ride down the 200 foot slide for $2.50 per person.

When you've worked up an appetite, the Wisconsin Expo Center offers higher-quality

34

local fare like Door County cherry products and artisan jerky, as well as kid favorites like grilled cheese and pizza. But the more traditional fair food, and the more adventurous options, lie outside.

The Machine Shed will usually satisfy the latter, serving up the likes of donut cheeseburgers and deep fried peanut butter and jelly sandwiches. For old favorites, search for pork chops and corn on the cob, capped off with a cream puff.

Other areas to visit that are sure to offer plenty of fun for the kids are the WE Energies Energy Park, the K-9 Sports Arena, and the Farm and Family Building.

Helpful Hints:
-Check the State Fair's website for Kohl's Family Value Day, when all fairgoers receive discounted admission.

-Children five and under are free throughout the fair.

-Get a free identification wristband for your children near a main entrance or at We Energies Energy Park.

-Save money on food on Crazy Grazin' Day. Check their website for details about vendors and specials.

Taste of the Islands
August

Marcus Center for the Performing Arts
929 N. Water St.,
Milwaukee, WI 53202
(414) 273-7121
marcuscenter.org/shows/live-at-peck

The annual Taste of the Islands event at the Marcus Center for the Performing Arts celebrates the ending of the Live at Peck Pavilion series. It focuses on a different island each year and includes live music and entertainment, themed food and beverages, and activities for kids such as crafts and face painting.

Farmer's Markets

Enjoying local Wisconsin goods and produce is one of the many perks of living here. Many of the following markets offer live music, kids' activities and free samples. It's the perfect way to while away a summer or early fall day.

Top pick: Cathedral Square Market
June-October
Saturdays, 9:00 a.m. - 1:00 p.m.
Cathedral Square Park
520 E Wells St.,
Milwaukee, WI 53202
easttown.com
Peruse fresh produce, locally made crafts, prepared foods, live entertainment and family-friendly activities. Over 100 Wisconsin farmers, craftsmen, bakers and chefs offer seasonal, fresh, and unique items. Everything is made or grown locally. Past activities include outdoor yoga, live local music and dance lessons for all ages.

Top pick: Fondy Market
May-November
Saturdays, 9:00 a.m. - 3:00 p.m.
2200 W. Fond Du Lac Ave,
Milwaukee, WI 53206
(414) 933-8121
The Fondy Farmers Market recently celebrated 100 years, and it is instrumental in ensuring a supply of healthy food to the city's north side. Tens of thousands of shoppers visit each year to enjoy an open-air market with live music and entertainment in addition to fresh produce.

Pro Tip: Don't miss the weekly "Seasonal Soul" cooking demonstration, featuring neighborhood chefs preparing nutritious soul food.

Top pick: Milwaukee Public Market Outdoor Urban Market
June-October
Saturdays, 10:00 a.m. - 3:00 p.m.
400 N. Water St.,
Milwaukee, WI 53202
(414) 336-1111
milwaukeepublicmarket.org
Located in Milwaukee's charming and unique Third Ward, the Urban Market offers fresh seasonal produce and regional artists. It's a farmer's market meets local art fair every weekend, and they often host live musicians, too.

Top pick: South Shore Farmer's Market

June-October
Saturdays, 8:00 a.m. - 12:00 p.m.
South Shore Park
2900 South Shore Dr.,
Milwaukee, WI 53027
southshorefarmersmarket.com
Enjoy stunning views of downtown and Lake Michigan from this farmer's market located in South Shore Park in funky Bay View. Besides the live music and local businesses, there's a playground and beer garden nearby.

Brown Deer Farmer's Market

June-October
Wednesdays, 9:00 a.m. - 6:00 p.m.
9078 N. Green Bay Rd.,
Brown Deer, WI 53209
browndeerfarmersmarket.org

Cedarburg Farmer's Market

June-October
Fridays, 9:00 a.m. - 2:00 p.m.
Mill & Washington
Cedarburg, WI 53012
cedarburg.org

Delafield Farmer's Market

May-October
Saturdays, 8:00 a.m - 1:00 p.m.
Fish Hatchery Building
417 Main St.,
Delafield, WI 53018
delafieldfarmersmarket.com

East Side Green Market

June-October
Saturdays, 10:00 a.m. - 2:00 p.m.
Beans and Barley parking lot
1901 E North Ave.,
Milwaukee, WI 53202
(414) 502-9489
theeastside.org

Fox Point Farmer's Market

June-October
Saturdays, 8:00 a.m. - 12:00 p.m.
7300 N. Lombardy Rd.,
Fox Point, WI 53217
(414) 352-0555
vil.fox-point.wi.us

Garden District Farmer's Market

June-October
Saturdays, 1:00 p.m. - 5:00 p.m.
6th Street and Howard Ave.,
Milwaukee, WI 53027
gardendistrictfarmersmarket.com

Greenfield Farmer's Market

June-October
Sundays, 10:00 a.m. - 2:00 p.m.
Konkel Park
5151 W Layton Ave.,
Greenfield, WI 53220
greenfieldfarmersmarket.com

New Berlin Farmer's Market

May-October
Saturdays, 8:00 a.m. - 12:00 p.m.
New Berlin Municipal Building
16300 W. National Ave.,
New Berlin, WI 53151
newberlinchamber.org

Oconomowoc Summer Farmer's Market
May-October
Saturdays, 7:00 a.m. - 12:00 p.m.
South Municipal Parking Lot
175 E Wisconsin Ave.,
Oconomowoc, WI 53066
oconomowoc.org

Tosa Farmer's Market
June-October
Saturdays, 8:00 a.m. - 12:00 p.m.
7720 Harwood Ave.,
Wauwatosa, WI 53213
(414) 301-2526
tosafarmersmarket.com

Walker Square Farmer's Market
June-October
Sundays, Tuesdays & Thursdays,
8:00 a.m. - 5:00 p.m.
Walker Square Park
Greenfield Ave. to the south,
the canal or Pierce/Bruce/
Virginia St. to the north, 6th
St. to the east and 16th St. to
the west
Milwaukee, WI 53204
walkersquare.org

Waukesha Farmer's Market
May-October
Saturdays, 8:00 a.m. - 12:00 p.m.
Historic Downtown Waukesha
in Riverfront Plaza
(Between Broadway
and Barstow)
Waukesha, WI 53086
waukeshafarmersmarket.com

West Allis Farmer's Market
May-November
Tuesdays and Thursdays,
12:00 p.m. - 6:00 p.m.
Saturdays, 1:00 p.m. - 6:00 p.m.
6501 W. National Ave.,
West Allis, WI 53214
westalliswi.gov

West Town Farmer's Market
June–October
Wednesdays, 10:00 a.m. - 3:00 p.m.
Zeidler Union Square
301 W. Michigan St.,
Milwaukee, WI 53203
(414) 257-7275
westown.org

milwaukee WITH KIDS

Golf & Miniature Golf

Helman's Driving Range & Mini-Golf ($)
N56W19901 Silver Spring Dr.,
Menomonee Falls, WI 53051
(262) 252-4447
helmansdrivingrange.com
Visit this seasonal outdoor sports center to play their 18-hole mini-golf course, practice on the driving range, or perfect your baseball swing in their batting cages.

Milwaukee County Parks / The First Tee of Southeast Wisconsin ($$$)
11350 W. Theodore Trecker Way,
West Allis, Wisconsin 53214
(414) 443-3570
thefirstteesoutheastwisconsin.org
Milwaukee County Parks partners with The First Tee and others to offer a huge selection of junior golf opportunities throughout the county starting at age seven. The parks offer beginner lessons, PGA Junior Leagues for kids 13 and under, and competitive golf tournaments. Programs have been offered at Brown Deer Park, Dretzka Park, and Noyes Park.

Moorland Golf Center ($)
5900 S. Moorland Rd.,
New Berlin, WI 53151
(262) 784-7552
moorlandgolfcenter.com
Moorland Golf Center's 18-hole mini-golf course features a coal mine, Farmer Ray's barn, a moon man, and a wizard. You'll be challenged by ponds, creeks, sand traps, and rock walls. After you work up your appetite, you can purchase a local treat like Cedar Crest ice cream, Sprecher root beer, Johnsonville Bratwurst, and more.

Prairieville Park ($)
2507 Plaza Ct.,
Waukesha, WI 53186
(262) 784-4653
prairievillepark.com
This seasonal family entertainment center houses five batting cages including slow-pitch softball, fast-pitch softball, and baseball from 35 to 80 miles per hour. There's also an adventure-style 18-hole mini-golf course with water features and a mountain, and bumper cars for kids taller than 44 inches.

River Falls Family Fun Center ($)

5401 W. Layton Ave.,
Greenfield, WI 53220
(414) 281-2815
riverfallsfamilyfuncenter.com
River Falls Family Fun Center
is home to outdoor activities
including mini-golf, batting
cages, and pedal karts. It's open
seasonally from April to October.

Swing Time ($)

swingtimegolf.com
Germantown location
W197 N10340 Appleton Ave.,
Germantown WI 53022
(262) 251-3311
Their 18-hole miniature golf
course has three waterfalls and a
70 foot hole, one of the longest in
the country. For extra fun, try the
19th hole for a chance to win one
free game. You'll also find batting
cages and go-karts for ages four
and up, with a minimum height
requirement of 36 inches.
Waukesha location
1601 E. Main St.,
Waukesha, WI 53186
(262) 547-3232
Miniature golf, batting cages,
and driving range.

Tee Aire Golf ($)

21700 Gumina Rd.,
Brookfield, WI 53072
(262) 781-2640
teeairegolf.com
Tee Air Golf has a beautifully
landscaped 18-hole miniature
golf course on artificial turf
greens, and they have putters for
kids as young as two years old.

A.W.E. inc.

Free Art For Kids!

This week in the Park
www.awe-inc.org   933-3877

Concert Series

Every night of the week in the summer, Milwaukee offers free live music for the whole family.

Top pick: Chill on the Hill (*)
Tuesdays, June-September
6:00-9:00 p.m.
Humboldt Park Bandshell
3000 S. Howell Ave.,
Milwaukee, WI 53207
(414) 257-8005
bayviewneighborhood.org
Chill on the Hill is the quintessential summer experience in Milwaukee's eclectic Bay View neighborhood. Head to the bandshell in beautiful Humboldt Park and enjoy local bands from your favorite spot on the hill. It feels like a neighborhood party with food trucks, activities for kids, pets, picnickers, and a generally festive vibe. (above)

Helpful hint: The playground and beer garden are just steps away, as well as a picturesque lagoon and walking paths.

Top Pick: Skyline Music Series (*)
Tuesdays, July-August
5:30 - 8:30 p.m.
Kadish Park
750 E. North Ave.,
Milwaukee, WI 53212
Riverwest's popular free concert series is presented by COA Youth and Family Centers, ensuring their weekly events are truly kid-friendly. Pack a picnic or enjoy food from one of the vendors, and enjoy the fantastic view of the river and Milwaukee skyline from the hill in Kadish Park. This concert series features a mix of jazz, soul, funk, and reggae musicians.

Don't miss it! Check out the kids' art corner featuring giveaways, crafts, activities, and surprises.

Top pick: Wonderful Wednesdays (*)

Wednesdays, July-August
6:30-7:30 p.m.
2975 N. Lake Park Rd.,
Milwaukee, WI 53211
(414) 962-1680
lakeparkfriends.org
Held in beautiful Lake Park, this is the only concert series designed especially for kids and their families. Enjoy local kids' bands such as the upbeat folk duo Fox and Branch, plenty of audience interaction, and lots of dancing. There is an indoor space available in case of inclement weather, so the concerts go on rain or shine.

Top pick: Concerts in the Gardens (*)

Thursdays, June-August
Boerner Botanical Gardens
9400 Boerner Dr.,
Hales Corners, WI 53130
wimmercommunities.com
Not only do you get to enjoy live music, but admission to the gardens to attend the summer concerts is free after 6:00 p.m. Visitors can walk through the gardens afterward at no additional cost. You can pack a picnic or purchase food and beverages on site.

Musical Mondays (*)

Mondays, July-August
Lake Park
2975 N. Lake Park Rd.,
Milwaukee, WI 53211
(414) 962-1680
lakeparkfriends.org

River Rhythms (*)

Wednesdays, June-August
Pere Marquette Park
900 N. Plankinton Ave.,
Milwaukee, WI 53203
(414) 276-6696
westown.org

Live at the Lakefront (*)

Wednesdays, July-September
Discovery World
500 N. Harbor Dr.,
Milwaukee, WI 53202
liveatthelakefront.com

Waterfront Wednesdays (*)

Wednesdays, June-August
Lakefront Park
222 W. Wisconsin Ave.,
Pewaukee, WI 53072
waterfrontwednesday.com

Jazz in the Park (*)

Thursdays, June-September
Cathedral Square Park
520 E. Wells St.,
Milwaukee, WI 53202
(414) 271-1416
eastown.com

Starry Night Series (*)

Fridays, June-August
Sharon Lynne Wilson
Center for the Arts
19805 W Capitol Dr.,
Brookfield, WI 53045
(262) 781-9520
wilson-center.com

Summer Sounds (*)

Fridays, June-August
Cedar Creek Park
N55 W6079 Portland Rd.,
Cedarburg, WI 53012
summersounds.net

Tosa Tonight (*)

Select Wednesdays, June - August
Rotary Park Pavilion
1190 N 70th St.,
Wauwatosa, WI 53213
(414) 395-0293
tosatonight.com

Traveling Tunes (*)

June – August
Thursdays, 6:30 p.m. - 8:30 p.m.
county.milwaukee.gov

Washington Park Wednesdays (*)

July – August
4145 W. Lisbon Ave.,
Milwaukee, WI 53208
county.milwaukee.gov

Waukesha Friday Night Live (*)

Fridays, June - October
Downtown Waukesha
W. Main St.,
Waukesha, WI 53186
waukeshafridaynightlive.com

Family Flicks (*)

county.milwaukee.gov
Milwaukee County Parks offer free family movie nights throughout the summer. They are held in a variety of parks including Veterans Park, Humboldt Park, and Grant Park on the beach. Check their website for the most up to date schedule.

Explore the RiverWalk (*)

visitmilwaukee.org/riverwalk/artwalk
Did you know that the RiverWalk in Milwaukee is actually an outdoor art gallery? It's called RiverSculpture, and it includes a mixture of permanent pieces and temporary installations.

You'll find polka dot stone benches, a whimsical and colorful statue called "Cow and Ballerina," and many more eye-catching sculptures.

Here are some highlights to look for:

-Located just off of Wells St. on the Milwaukee RiverWalk, the Bronze Fonz is Milwaukee's ultimate selfie destination. The statue is a tribute to Arthur Fonzareli from "Happy Days," a sitcom based in Milwaukee circa 1950. The statue is five foot six, just like the actor who played the Fonz, Henry Winkler.

-Don't miss Gertie the Duck! In April of 1945, a mallard duck nested under the Wisconsin Avenue Bridge. A story in the Milwaukee Journal dubbed her "Gertie," and it went viral in a 1940's kind of way. Crowds gathered and motorists stopped by the nest to check on the ducklings' status. It captivated Milwaukee and eventually the entire nation.

Five ducklings eventually hatched, and the ducks were put on display in Gimbel's department store. The ducks were later relocated to the Juneau Park lagoon.

Today Gertie the Duck stands guard over her ducklings in all their bronze glory on the Wisconsin Avenue Bridge over the Milwaukee River. The sculpture by Gwendolyn Gillen was installed in 1997.

Airplane Spotting (*)

1200 block of E. Layton Ave. If your kids love airplanes, the Airport Observation Area is a sure-fire hit. Aviation buffs and amateur onlookers flock to this parking lot on the 1200 block of E. Layton Ave. to get an up-close look and hear the roar of the massive jet planes as they come and go. Tune into 88.5 to hear aircraft communication. You can pick up some Culver's custard down the road, sit out on the car hood and make a night of it.

Kids Bowl Free (*)

kidsbowlfree.com
To stay cool and have free fun in the summertime, register your child on kidsbowlfree.com. Registered children get two free games of bowling every single day of the summer. Check the website for a participating bowling alley near you.

Marcus Center Kidz Days (*)

Marcus Center for the Performing Arts
929 N. Water St.,
Milwaukee, WI 53202
(414) 273-7121
marcuscenter.org
Marcus Center Kidz Days offers live, interactive, performing arts programming for kids completely free every Tuesday, Wednesday & Thursday from the end of June through the middle of August. Partners include First Stage Theater, Rick Allen Magic Show, Milwaukee Public Library, Betty Brinn Children's Museum, Trinity Irish Dancers, Milwaukee Ballet, Wehr Nature Center, and Lucky's African Drumming.

Live at Peck (*)

Marcus Center for the Performing Arts
929 N. Water St.,
Milwaukee, WI 53202
(414) 273-7121
marcuscenter.org
The Live at Peck series includes free Sunday Band concerts, free Peck Flicks, and Tuesday Dance Competitions. During DanceMKE, selected performance groups dance for cash, trophies and glory over the course of a few weeks, and the public is invited to watch the exciting competitions.

Waterski Shows (*)

Badgerland Waterski Show
badgerland.org

Wednesday Evenings,
Memorial Day to Labor Day,
7:00 p.m.
Frame Park on the Fox River
1150 Frame Park Dr.,
Waukesha, WI 53186

Thursday Evenings,
Memorial Day to Labor Day,
7:00 p.m.
Fowler Park on Fowler Lake
500 Oakwood Ave.,
Oconomowoc, WI 53066

Pewaukee Lake Water Ski Club
Thursday evenings,
Memorial Day to Labor Day,
6:45 p.m.
Lakefront Park
222 W. Wisconsin Ave.,
Pewaukee, WI 53072
plwsc.org

Gift of Wings Kite Festivals (*)

1300 N. Lincoln Memorial Dr.,
Milwaukee, WI 53202
(414) 273-5483
The Gift of Wings kite store located in Veterans Park sells kites of all kinds (and ice cream), but they also host free events for families all year round. Check their website for more information about their annual kite festivals over Labor Day weekend, Fourth of July, Memorial Day weekend, and New Year's Day. The festivals include a grand launch of vibrantly colored kites, live music, food, and fun flies.

Autumn

Apple Picking

Top pick: Peck and Bushel Fruit Company

5472 County Road Q,
Colgate, WI 53017
(414) 418-0336
peckandbushel.com

Just a 35 minute drive from the hustle and bustle of the city, Peck and Bushel Fruit Company is the Milwaukee area's only organic apple orchard. Their property is picturesque and serene without any of the loud bells and whistles of some of the other orchards. Purchase your pick-your-own bags in the country store, which houses a bakery, jarred jams and apple butters, and autumn-themed home decor. You'll walk past a peaceful pond and along a tree covered nature path towards the orchard. There's a swing and walking bridge perfect for family pictures. The owners, Joe and Jennifer Fahey, grow their apples vineyard style, and they seem to add new varieties every year. You'll never eat a honey crisp apple that tastes better than theirs. At the end of your visit, you can enjoy your treats on their new patio overlooking the pond.

Top pick: Nieman Orchards

9932 Pioneer Rd.,
Cedarburg, WI 53012
(262) 377-4284
niemanorchards.com

The "Old Red Barn" is rustic and filled with Neiman Orchards' own products, such as their delicious homemade cider. Purchase your picking bags inside the barn, or use one of their vintage wooden baskets to collect your fruit. Behind the farm, an old fashioned

46

wagon will take you on a short ride out to the orchard. You can wander rows and rows of apple trees, picking what you fancy, seeing nothing else but crops in any direction. Besides apples, Neiman Orchards also offers pick-your-own pumpkins in September and October.

Apple Barn Orchard and Winery

W. 6384 Sugar Creek Rd.,
Elkhorn, WI 53121
(262) 728-3266
applebarnorchardandwinery.com

This real family farm experience is a memorable one. Delight in the beautiful landscape, wildflowers, and fresh air as you pick your own apples from their orchard. Their lovely country store offers seasonal products from their farm. A visit here is a feast for the senses.

Helpful Hint: Don't get confused! Apple Barn Orchard and Winery is located on Sugar Creek <u>Road</u> with one of the cross streets being Sugar Creek <u>Street</u>.

Apple Holler

5006 S. Sylvania Ave.,
Sturtevant, WI 53177
(262) 884-7100
appleholler.com

Apple Holler is a popular spot for families in the fall, so expect crowds. They offer pick-your-own apples of many varieties. Your kids can also explore the Farm Park, including a corn maze, an animal feeding area, pony rides, tractor tours, and a giant slide. Pumpkins are available in October.

Awe's Apple Orchard

8081 S. 100th St.,
Franklin, WI 53132
(414) 425-1426

To the south of the city, nestled on a little pond along Highway 100 in the city of Franklin, you'll spot Awe's Apple Orchard. Even the gravel path leading to the main orchard area is lined with beautiful apple trees to entice you. You'll drive past the quaint pond, enormous old trees, and fall-themed scarecrows. Adjacent to the parking lot, you'll spot the store and the white tent where you purchase your apple picking bags. Awe's Orchard is not huge, but it's smaller size contributes to its charm. They offer McIntosh, Golden Delicious and Honeycrisp apples, and a sizable pumpkin patch. Don't miss their homemade apple cider donuts. They are fried and crispy on the outside, and perfectly soft on the inside. It's the perfect way to reward yourself for all that rigorous apple picking you did. You can visit the "apple house" for fresh picked apples, apple cider, apple crisp mix, jams, and more.

Barthel Fruit Farm

12246 N. Farmdale Rd.,
Mequon, WI 53097
(262) 242-2737
barthelfruitfarm.com
Far from strip malls and city life, Barthel Fruit Farm is expansive, and their apple-picking process is a well-oiled machine. The drive-by attendant will provide you with all the information you need, as well as the bags for picking. Pay on the way out at their drive-through register. If you want to pick up a caramel apple to end the experience, you can park off to the right before you exit and visit the store. Inquire about their plum orchard, which felt pretty magical on the foggy day we visited. You'll feel as though you're walking through a fairy tale as you roam through rows of plum trees bursting with blue and purple ripened plums ready for the picking. Barthel Fruit Farm offers pumpkins later in the season, too.

Basse's Country Delight

S70W16050 Janesville Rd.,
Muskego, WI 53150
(414) 422-0315
bassescountrydelight.com
Enjoy sweet corn, apples, pumpkins, plus a hayride, petting zoo, and country store.

Elegant Farmer

1545 Main St.,
Mukwonago, WI 53149
(262) 363-6770
elegantfarmer.com
You can spot the smiley farm from a mile away. Elegant Farmer's popular Harvest Fest runs on weekends in September and October. Pick a variety of apples and pumpkins, hop on a hayride (or a pony), make your own caramel apple, explore the corn maze, and enjoy their delicious cider donuts. You can also catch the vintage East Troy Electric Railcar from here.

Patterson Orchards

4607 S. 124th St.,
New Berlin, Wisconsin 53151
(414) 425-0563
Customers rave about the caramel apples offered at Patterson Orchards.

Rim's Edge Orchard

W220N10550 Amy Belle Rd.,
Colgate, WI 53017
(262) 509-0090
rimsedgeorchard.com
Though your GPS might be confused by the address, this orchard is located at the corner of Amy Belle and Willow Creek roads. You'll find over 20 varieties of apples, pick-your-own options, plus local syrups and honey in the store.

Weston's Antique Apples

19760 W. National Ave.,
New Berlin, WI 53146
(262) 501-9223
westonapples.com
While you're not able to pick-your-own apples from the antique trees, you can take your children on an orchard tour of this fascinating place. This family-owned orchard is owned by Ken Weston. The farm began

48

in 1936 when his grandfather planted apples over 11 acres. They planted varieties that were prevalent in the 1930's but are now antiques. Some varieties go all the way back to 300 AD. According to Ken, some don't even taste like apples.

The historic property looks exactly the way it did in the 1930's, and it's on the National Register of Historic Landscapes. It's the oldest active orchard in Waukesha County.

Helpful Hint: You can also visit Weston's Antique Apples by attending AppleFest on the first Sunday of October each year. It features lots of family-friendly fun including barrel train rides, pioneer homes and buildings to tour, apple cider making, square dancing in the barn, and more old-fashioned fun.

Pumpkin Patches and Fall Fun

Many of the apple orchards listed in the previous section also offer pumpkins.

Best Corn Maze: Schuett Farms ($)
W299 S6370 Hwy 83, Mukwonago, WI 53149
(262) 968-4348
schuettfarm.com
Schuett Farm's corn maze is nine acres and boasts over three miles of pathways. You can actually use your smartphone to navigate and search for designated checkpoints. They also offer a night time maze. Flashlights are required and it is not haunted, but beware - it gets muddy!

Best for little kids: Swan Pumpkin Farm ($$)
5930 Highway H, Franksville, WI 53126
(262) 835-4885
thepumpkinfarm.com
Buy pre-picked pumpkins and gourds and enjoy a corn maze, live theater, petting zoo, tractor-pulled hayrides and more.

Giant pumpkins: Land of the Giants Pumpkin Farm ($)

11823 Highway 11,
Sturtevant, WI 53177
(262) 886-6690
giantpumpkinfarm.com
Have you ever seen a giant pumpkin up close before? Head to this pumpkin farm to see just that, plus choose from an assortment of pre-picked pumpkins, gourds and squash, and experience the corn maze, tractor-pulled hay rides, wagon rides, a petting zoo and more.

Basse's Taste of Country Farm Market ($$)

3190 County Line Rd.,
Colgate WI 53017
(262) 628-2626
bassesfarms.com
Hop on a hayride out to one of the largest pumpkin farms around. They offer dozens of fun fall activities for the whole family including an eight acre corn maze, pig races, tractor pull, giant slides, ropes course, and more.

Bear Den Zoo and Petting Farm ($)

6831 Big Bend Rd.,
Waterford, WI 53185
(262) 895-6430
beardenzoo.com
The admission price to Bear Den Zoo & Petting Farm includes a hayride through the woods, access to the petting zoo and baby animal petting areas, and exploration in the children's play area.

Borzynski's Farm & Floral Market ($)

11600 Washington Ave.,
Mt. Pleasant, WI 53177
(262) 886-2235
borzynskis.com
Pumpkins are available in the market, and you can also explore a themed corn maze (bring a flashlight for night time!), hop on a hay ride, make your own caramel apple, pet the animals in the petting zoo, and more.

Cedarburg Creek Farm ($)

649 Hwy 60,
Cedarburg, WI 53012
(262) 894-6624
cedarburgcreekfarm.com
Enjoy free admission and free hay rides to this pick-your-own pumpkin patch. Be prepared to pay for the other activities you want to participate in, including bouncy houses and a barrel train. There is also a petting zoo and pony rides.

Cozy Nook Farm ($)

W30780 Summit Ave.,
Waukesha, WI 53188
(262) 968-2573
cozynookfarms.com
Visit this real working family farm, and take a hay ride out to the pick-your-own pumpkin patch. Be on the lookout - You may spot a cow on your journey!

Creekside Valley Farm ($)

13101 N Wauwatosa Rd.,
Mequon, WI 53097
(414) 852-5752
creeksidevalleyfarm.com
This farm offers pick-your-own

pumpkins, a corn maze, a petting zoo, peddle tractors, pumpkin games, fall decor, plus a theater room with fall themed movies & free popcorn. (Yes, they play Packer games in the theater room on Sundays.)

Homestead Animal Farm ($)

W320 N9127 Highway 83, Hartland, WI 53029
(262) 966-3840
homesteadanimalfarm.com
Buy already picked pumpkins, gourds, squash, Indian corn and more. Have fun in the corn maze, enjoy tractor-pulled hay rides, and meet the farm animals.

Jim's Pumpkin Farm ($)

N124W17781 Lovers Ln., Germantown, WI 53022
(262) 251-0463
jimspumpkinfarm.com
Pick your own pumpkins or choose from already picked pumpkins, Indian corn, gourds and more. Take a hayride or get lost in the corn maze.

Lindners Pumpkin Farm and Corn Maze ($)

19075 W. Cleveland Ave., New Berlin, WI 53146
(262) 549-5364
lindnerspumpkinfarm.com
This pumpkin farm offers a Pumpkin Express Barrel Train, carnival and fall-themed games, a giant slide, and an old-fashioned playground. Explore the petting zoo with goats, mini-pigs, llama, mini-horse, and bunnies, plus a Big Backyard play area. You can also tour an 1840's log cabin. For the especially brave ones, the corn maze is haunted at night.

Meadowbrook Pumpkin Farm ($)

2970 Mile View Rd., West Bend, WI 53095
(262) 338-3649
meadowbrookfun.com
Pick your own pumpkins or buy already picked pumpkins. You can also check out their corn maze, haunted corn maze, tractor-pulled hay rides, wagon rides, petting zoo, farm animals and more.

Prospect Hill Garden Center ($)

19305 W. National Ave., New Berlin, WI 53146
(262) 679-2207
bloomssite.com
Take a hayride to the pumpkin patch and enjoy a corn maze, petting zoo, lots of games for kids, face painting, and food.

Witte's Vegetable Farm ($)

10006 Bridge Rd., Cedarburg, WI 53012
(262) 377-1423
wittesvegfarm.com
Bring your own containers and get ready to pick some farm fresh vegetables. In the fall, pick your own pumpkins or buy already picked pumpkins, gourds and Indian corn. They also offer raw honey and maple syrup.

Not-so-scary Halloween Annual Events

Nightmare Before Christmas (*)
facebook.com/NBCBayview
For a spooky treat, drive down to the 2700 block of Logan Street in Milwaukee's Bay View neighborhood around Halloween time. You'll find elaborate and illuminated Halloween decorations with a Nightmare Before Christmas theme.

Boo at the Zoo & Halloween Spooktacular ($$)
Milwaukee County Zoo
10001 W. Bluemound Rd.,
Milwaukee, WI 53226
(414) 771-3040
milwaukeezoo.org
The Milwaukee County Zoo hosts special fall events in October. Boo at the Zoo typically includes a haystack maze, bat exhibits, caramel apples, a pumpkin patch, light shows, spooky story times, and a haunted train ride. The Halloween Spooktacular features trick-or-treating throughout the zoo.

Halloween Haunts ($)
Wehr Nature Center
9701 W. College Ave.,
Franklin, WI 53132
(414) 425-8550
friendsofwehr.org
Halloween Haunts is designed especially for families with children ages four to ten. Wehr's wooded area is transformed into an Enchanted Forest filled with Happy Halloween characters like glowing mushrooms. After the hike, visitors can enjoy cider, popcorn, games, crafts, face painting, magic shows, and more.

52

Halloween Glen ($)

Hawthorn Glen
Nature Center
1130 N. 60th St.,
Milwaukee, WI 53208
(414) 647-6050

This humorous and educational outdoor adventure is a great way to incorporate nature into your Halloween celebration with your family. Actors present interactive skits along the lighted trails of Hawthorn Glen, Milwaukee Recreation's 23-acre nature center. Families can then make craft projects, watch Halloween cartoons, and enjoy refreshments. This event is best for ages 3-12.

Haunted Sullivan ($)

Discovery World
500 N. Harbor Dr.,
Milwaukee, WI 53202
(414) 765-9966
discoveryworld.org

Discovery World's tall ship, the S/V Denis Sullivan, is the world's only recreation of a 19th century three-masted Great Lakes schooner. Every Halloween it is transformed into a not-too-spooky haunted tall ship hosted by the captain and crew. Tours are 20 minutes long.

Haunted Halloween on Downer Avenue (*)

downeravenue.com

The businesses on Historic Downer Avenue invite families to trick-or-treat each Halloween. They invite chalk artists and provide other family-friendly activities and prizes at this free event.

Not-so-scary Halloween ($)

Betty Brinn
Children's Museum
929 E. Wisconsin Ave.,
Milwaukee, WI 53202
(414) 390-5437
bbcmkids.org

Each year the Betty Brinn Children's Museum hosts a Halloween celebration for young kids. It includes treat stops throughout the museum sponsored by local businesses, plus Halloween themed activities in their Be a Maker space. The event is always free with museum admission.

Pumpkin Pavilion (*)

Humboldt Park Pavilion
3000 S. Howell Ave.,
Milwaukee, WI 53207
(414) 257-7275
bayviewneighborhood.org

Bay View's signature Halloween festival features hundreds of intricately carved pumpkins, illuminated and displayed at the Humboldt Park Pavilion. Families can enjoy hay rides, live bands, an old black and white movie for spooky ambiance, and other kid-friendly activities. Don't miss the magical Grand Lighting!

Retzer Howl-O-Ween: An Unhaunted Halloween Event ($)

Retzer Nature Center
S14 W28167 Madison St.,
Waukesha, WI 53188
(262) 896-8007
waukeshacounty.gov

Each year in October, Retzer Nature Center hosts this family-friendly event recommended for children 10 and under. They host an unhaunted barn dance, owl prowl hike, campfire stories and children's activity areas. Coming dressed in costumes is encouraged.

Whitefish Bay Great Pumpkin Festival (*)

Old Schoolhouse Park
5420 N. Marlborough Dr.,
Whitefish Bay, WI 53217
wfbcivicfoundation.org

The Whitefish Bay Civic Foundation presents this pumpkin festival each year in Old Schoolhouse Park. They provide free pumpkins, carving tools, candles, and tables. Families can design a jack-o-lantern that will be lit and on display each night of the festival. There is also live music and local food.

milwaukee
WITH KIDS

Día de los Muertos events

Día de los Muertos (Day of the Dead) is a festival steeped in indigenous Mexican tradition. It honors and celebrates loved ones who have passed. Celebrations are meaningful, emotional, and at times even light-hearted and humorous. It often features colorful floral arrangements, photographs, and skeleton iconography. To learn more about the festival or to join in the celebration, check out these events and exhibits.

Día de los Muertos Festival (*)
October
Walkers Square Park
1031 S. 9th St.,
Milwaukee, WI 53204
(414) 257-7275
diadelosmuertosmilwaukee.com
Milwaukee's biggest Day of the Dead celebration features a parade, art market, live DJ, Aztec dancers, traditional ofrendas (altars dedicated to loved ones who have passed away), food trucks, and more.

Día de los Muertos exhibit at Walkers Point Center for the Arts (*)
October - November
839 S. 5th St.,
Milwaukee, WI 53204
(414) 672-2787
wpca-milwaukee.org
Each year, WPCA presents colorful artwork and ofrendas (altars), traditionally decorated with items like sugar skulls, flowers, papel picado (literally "chopped paper"), as well as personal items of loved ones who have passed.

Latino Arts, Inc. Day of the Dead celebration ($)
October - November
1028 S. 9th St.,
Milwaukee, WI 53204
(414) 384-3100
latinoartsinc.org
The Latino Arts' Gallery is open to the public for its annual Day of the Dead celebration, featuring a bright and eclectic collection of ofrendas (altars) prepared by local, regional, and international artists. Artists present their tributes to loved ones who have passed away in celebration of their lives.

Annual Fall Festivals

Harvest Fair (*)

Wisconsin State Fair Grounds
640 S. 84th St.,
West Allis, WI 53214
(414) 266-7000
wistatefair.com
Enjoy autumnal activities such as a kiddie tractor maze, hay rides, camel and pony rides, cookie decorating, fall-themed arts and crafts, make-your-own caramel apple stands, pumpkin bowling and decorating, scarecrow making, plus live music.

Sturgeon Fest (*)

Lakeshore State Park
500 N. Harbor Dr.,
Milwaukee, WI 53202
(414) 274-4281
sturgeonfest.org
Sturgeon Fest is one of the biggest annual conservation events and festivals in Wisconsin, and its mission is to return a breeding population of Sturgeon to Lake Michigan and the Milwaukee River. Activities for families typically include kayak demonstrations, prairie tours, educational booths, delicious local food trucks, and more.

Insider tip: The festival is free, but you can release your own sturgeon into Lake Michigan for an affordable donation.

Wine & Harvest Festival

September
Historic Downtown Cedarburg
cedarburgfestival.org
Kick off the autumn season at a family-oriented arts and crafts event in historic downtown Cedarburg. Enjoy live music all over downtown, hop aboard a tractor-drawn hayride wagon, explore a juried arts show, taste the original apple brat, watch the annual Giant Pumpkin Weigh-Off and Giant Pumpkin Charity Regatta, and visit the kid's area featuring clowns, art projects, pumpkin painting, and more. The Cedar Creek Winery's annual Kid's Grape Stomp is a daily crowd-pleaser.

New Berlin Applefest (*)

New Berlin Historical Park
19765 W. National Ave.,
New Berlin, WI 53146
(262) 643-8855
newberlinhistoricalsociety.org
Ride the orchard barrel train, check out the cider press, join square dancing in the barn, pick out a pumpkin, operate model trains in the museum, and more!

56

Fall Festival at Piala's Nursery (*)

S39W27833 Genesee Rd., Waukesha, WI 53189
(262) 547-2677
pialasnursery.com

All ages are welcome, and there is no charge for admission. The festival typically features a bouncy house, giant slide, games, live music, a craft fair with local artisans, hot food and beverages, visits to the Peacock Palace, pumpkin, squash and gourd carving, raffles, Waukesha Fire Department and Sheriff's vehicles, a ladder truck, meet and greets, and more.

Thiensville Applefest (*)

Thiensville Village Park
250 Elm St.,
Thiensville, WI 53092
(262) 242-3720
tmlions.org

Applefest is a celebration of the autumn harvest and Ozaukee County's apple heritage. Enjoy the charming small town atmosphere in a beautiful park on the shores of the Milwaukee River. The festival features live music, fresh apples and apple cider, and other fall fun such as hay rides, an apple pie baking contest, coloring contest, polka contest, big wheel racing, and face painting.

Oktoberfest (*)

Historic Downtown Cedarburg
cedarburgfestival.org

Cedarburg's annual Oktoberfest features authentic German music and dancers, a real wood floor for polka dancing, and a Glockenspiel Show (Cuckoo Clock). Enjoy German food and beverages including curry wurst, bratwurst, and sausage platters. There is even a sauerkraut eating contest, German spelling bee, and a Volkswagon Club car display.

Cider Sunday ($)

Wehr Nature Center
9701 W. College Ave.,
Franklin, WI 53132
(414) 425-8550
friendsofwehr.org

Enjoy an afternoon filled with live music, family activities, and fresh-made apple cider. Take a guided walk along the Nature Center trails and explore the changing colors of the season. You can even make cider with their hand crank cider press, or sample and learn how apple butter is made over an open fire. Plus, enjoy live bluegrass music, apple tasting, an old-fashioned cake walk, fall crafts, and more.

Family Farm Weekend ($$)

Milwaukee County Zoo
10001 W. Bluemound Rd.,
Milwaukee, WI 53226
(414) 771-3040
milwaukeezoo.org

Visit the Northwestern Mutual Family Farm for fun farm-related activities, including a basket weaving demonstration, a local farmers market featuring fresh, locally grown produce, and a milk chugging contest. Other activities include a pedal tractor-pull, the Wisconsin Spudmobile, and ice cream making demonstrations. All activities are free with regular Zoo admission.

Apple Harvest Festival ($)

Retzer Nature Center
S14W28167 Madison St.,
Waukesha, Wisconsin 53188
(262) 896-8007
waukeshacounty.gov

Enjoy arts & crafts, horse drawn wagon rides, planetarium shows, children's games and activities, live music, an apple market, and more.

Holiday Folk Fair ($$)

State Fair Park
Exposition Center
8200 W. Greenfield Ave.,
West Allis, Wisconsin 53214
(414) 727-8840
folkfair.org

Held every year in November, the Folk Fair is an exhilarating display of world cultures, music, dance, food, and artwork. The multicultural festival celebrates the diversity of over 50 ethnicities from African to Welsh. The colorful costumes, flavorful food, giant tipis, and lively music and dancing make this event one of the most memorable of the year.

Winter

Holiday Cheer

It's a magical time of year, especially for children, and Milwaukee is replete with festive ways to celebrate the season. Dazzling holiday light displays, themed train rides, breakfast with Santa, and exciting parades will make this Christmas the most enchanted one yet.

Tree Lightings & Parades

Annual City Christmas Tree Lighting (*)
City Hall
200 E. Wells St.,
Milwaukee, WI 53202
(414) 220-4700
milwaukeedowntown.com
This century-old tradition features uplifting music from local choirs, ensembles and theater groups, and a fun countdown to lighting up the city's evergreen tree. Afterwards, you can easily walk over the Kilbourn Avenue bridge to the Milwaukee Holiday Lights Festival Kick-Off Extravaganza in Pere Marquette Park.

Milwaukee Holiday Lights Festival Kick-Off Extravaganza (*)
Pere Marquette Park
900 N. Plankinton Ave.,
Milwaukee, WI 53203
(414) 220-4700
milwaukeedowntown.com
After the lighting of the city's holiday tree, Pere Marquette Park comes alive with a festive lights display, fireworks, a visit from Santa, and spirited holiday music and entertainment. After the show, attendees can take free Jingle Bus rides through downtown's newly illuminated displays.

Bayshore Town Center Tree Lighting & Celebration

5800 N. Bayshore Dr.,
Glendale, WI 53217
bayshoretowncenter.com
Join local choirs and welcome Santa as he turns on the tree lights in town square. Take a magical horse-drawn carriage ride and enjoy hot chocolate and cookies.

Christmas Parade in Downtown Waukesha (*)

waukeshaworks.com
The parade has been a holiday tradition for over half a century, bringing together local civic groups, businesses, schools, public services, and amateur and professional entertainers. It is held each year on the Sunday before Thanksgiving to officially begin the holiday season for thousands of spectators.

The Pfister Hotel's Annual Tree Lighting Event (*)

424 E. Wisconsin Ave.,
Milwaukee, WI 53202
(414) 273-8222
thepfisterhotel.com
The Pfister Hotel's tree lighting ceremony features an 18-foot LED lit holiday tree, complimentary holiday treats, music, hot cocoa, and more. Parents can snap pictures of their children with Santa and Mrs. Claus, and kids can write letters to Santa and send them in a special mailbox that goes straight to the North Pole.

Tree lighting at The Hilton Milwaukee Hotel (*)

509 W Wisconsin Ave.,
Milwaukee, WI 53203
(414) 271-7250
hiltonmilwaukee.com
If you're downtown for Milwaukee's annual holiday parade in November, head over to the Hilton Milwaukee City Center for their Christmas tree lighting following the parade. Indulge in complimentary hot chocolate and cookies, caroling, family-friendly activities, holiday movies around the fireplace, and pictures with Santa.

Christmas in the Ward (*)

Select weekend in December

Historic Third Ward

historicthirdward.org

The Historic Third Ward is a charming, upscale neighborhood just south of downtown. Each Christmas, you'll find a magical tree lighting in Catalano Square (which is actually a triangle shape - go figure), live reindeer, chestnuts roasting on an open fire (really!), horse drawn carriage rides, costumed characters, hot cocoa, and more. You can visit with Santa in Jolly's Outdoor Gingerbread House, too.

Don't miss it!

Look for the cocoa cocktails offered for the adults.

Whitefish Bay Holiday Stroll and Tree Lighting (*)

E. Silver Spring Dr.

wfbcivicfoundation.org

Held each year on the Friday following Thanksgiving, the Holiday Stroll includes an impressive parade, tree lighting ceremony, food, music, and more. Kids can also enjoy a free pony, train, or trolley ride, and visit Santa with his reindeer.

Annual West Allis Christmas Parade & Tree Lighting (*)

westalliswi.gov

This parade includes marching bands and live performers, impressive floats, vintage cars, elves and mascots, and of course, Santa Claus himself. The Parade kicks off at the State Fair Park entrance. You can also check out Christmas on the Avenue before the parade, featuring family activities, crafts, games, caroling and the annual Christmas tree lighting.

New Berlin Christmas Parade

newberlin.org

The parade typically starts at 159th Street and National Ave. proceeding to Al Stigler Parkway. A magical tree lighting ceremony follows the parade at Casper and National Ave.

Holiday Lights

Top pick:
Candy Cane Lane (*)
West Allis (Between 92nd and
96th St. and between Montana
and Oklahoma Ave.)
Late November - Late December
candycanelanewi.com
Candy Cane Lane (*above*) is the
perfect holiday tradition for any
family who loves Christmas lights.
Grab some hot cocoa to go, and
drive over to this brightly lit West
Allis neighborhood. You'll enter
to find a winter wonderland with
trees decorated like candy canes
and over 300 houses full of festive
holiday lights. You can drive or
walk through. Don't forget to leave
a donation for the MACC fund.

Milwaukee Holiday Lights & $1.00 Jingle Bus Tours (*)
Late November - late December
milwaukeedowntown.com
The annual six-week lights festival
throughout downtown Milwaukee
features animated holiday light
displays in Cathedral Square Park,
Pere Marquette Park and Zeidler
Union Square. You can get an up-
close look at the lights aboard the
$1.00 Jingle Bus, a Coach USA bus
that takes visitors on a 40-minute
tour narrated by Milwaukee
Downtown's Public Service
Ambassadors. Tours depart from
The Shops of Grand Avenue.
*Helpful Hint: While you wait, you
can enjoy holiday snacks and the
Leonard Bearstein Symphony,
comprised entirely of animated
stuffed bears, inside the mall.*

BMO Harris Bank Holiday Display (*)
770 N. Water St.,
Milwaukee, WI 53202
(414) 765-7500
bmoharris.com
Each year the lobby of the BMO

Harris Bank downtown turns into a holiday wonderland. There is a different theme each year, but it's always larger than life and worth a visit. The exhibit is free.

Lights on Glen Cove (*)

Off Janesville and Glen Cove Ct. in Muskego, WI

Marvel at over 35,000 LED lights synchronized to holiday music from 87.9 FM. The display raises money for charity, and runs every night starting at 5:00 p.m. until 9:00 p.m. on weekdays and 10:00 p.m. on weekends. This display is located in a residential neighborhood, so be sure to turn off your headlights and keep your radio at a low volume.

Country Springs Christmas Lights Display ($)

2810 Golf Rd.,
Pewaukee, WI 53072
(262) 547-0201
thecountrychristmas.com

Each year, the land just west of the Country Springs Hotel transforms into a wooded winter wonderland called Country Christmas. Your admission will enable you to drive through the one-mile long Country Christmas Trail, which features over a million holiday lights. Kids will love "Bearville" with its giant teddy bears running errands in the general store and going to church. The highlight of the lights show is an other-worldly drive through a 200-foot tunnel of 30,000 twinkling lights. At the end of the drive, you can hop out of the car and walk through the Streets of Bethlehem, where you'll find an almost life-sized replica of the Fontanini nativity scene found at the Vatican. You can also explore Christmas Village, featuring model trains, an area to take photos, and concessions.

Enchantment in the Park ($)

Regner Park
800 N. Main St.,
West Bend, WI 53090
enchantmentpark.org

This huge twinkling lights display in Regner Park is impressive for all ages. You can walk, drive, or take a carriage ride through, and Santa is there to visit with the kids. It gets very busy on the weekends, so visit during the week if you can. Bring a bag of non-perishable food items or $10 cash donation.

Miller Valley Holiday Lites (*)

4251 W. State St.,
Milwaukee, WI 53208
(414) 931-BEER (2337)
millercoors.com

Drive through the historic Miller Valley at Christmas time and you'll find a new holiday lights display each year. The illuminated valley comes alive with over half a million LED lights synchronized to music. The theme changes each year, and it's totally free to drive through. They also offer free brewery tours.

Breakfasts with Santa

Breakfast with Santa at the Milwaukee County Zoo ($$$)
Select weekends in December
10001 W. Bluemound Rd.,
Milwaukee, WI 53226
milwaukeezoo.org
Each year, Santa and Mrs. Claus, along with their elves, make their annual trip to the Milwaukee County Zoo to visit children for a special breakfast or lunch. Enjoy live holiday carols and a special gift for each child.

Breakfast with Santa at the Hilton ($$$)
509 W. Wisconsin Ave.,
Milwaukee, WI 53203
(414) 271-7250
hiltonmilwaukee.com
Share a jolly breakfast with Santa and his elves in the Hilton's ballroom, decorated as a Christmas wonderland. Kids can build and decorate a keepsake ornament, get their face painted, watch a holiday movie, and get a special gift.

Breakfast with Santa at the Pfister ($$$)
424 E. Wisconsin Ave.,
Milwaukee, WI 53202
(414) 273-8222
thepfisterhotel.com
Kids can enjoy a festive breakfast with Santa and his elves in The Pfister's ballroom. Each child will get a special gift from Santa.

Breakfast with Santa Downtown Waukesha ($$)
Saturdays in December
Martha Merrell's Books
231 W Main St.,
Waukesha, WI 53186
downtownwaukesha.com
Enjoy breakfast with Santa at Martha Merrell's Books and Toy Store throughout the holiday season. They offer delicious hot breakfast with juice and cookies, and arts & crafts with Santa himself.

Annual Holiday Shows

The Nutcracker at the Marcus Center for the Performing Arts ($$$)

Various showtimes throughout December

Marcus Center for the Performing Arts
929 N.Water St.,
Milwaukee, WI 53202
(414) 273-7121
marcuscenter.org

Each year, take a dazzling journey to a magical land where dolls, toys and snowflakes come to life under the direction of Tchaikovsky's unforgettable score. The Milwaukee Ballet Orchestra performs alongside the Milwaukee Children's Choir, and it's an undeniably magnificent performance.

Holiday Pajama Jamboree (*)

Marcus Center for the Performing Arts
929 N.Water St.,
Milwaukee, WI 53202
(414) 365-8861
festivalcitysymphony.org

Every winter, the Festival City Symphony offers this free classical pops concert, one hour in length and geared towards children and their families. Each concert has narration, lively music selections, and a kid-friendly atmosphere. There are frequently dancers, costumed actors, children's performing groups, and sometimes audience members even get to conduct. Kids are encouraged to wear their pajamas, and teddy bears and blankets are welcome. Snuggle up in a spot on the floor directly in front of the orchestra.

A Christmas Carol ($$$)

Milwaukee Repertory Theater
108 E. Wells St.,
Milwaukee, WI 53202
(414) 224-9490
milwaukeerep.com

A Milwaukee holiday tradition for over four decades, this show is a classic tale of love and redemption, mixed with lively music, dancing, and special effects. It's about two hours long including intermission, and is perfect for kids ages six and up.

More Holiday Events

Cocoa with the Clauses (*)

Cathedral Square Park
520 E. Wells St.,
Milwaukee, WI 53202
(414) 220-4700
milwaukeedowntown.com

Cocoa with the Clauses is one of the highlights of the Milwaukee Holiday Lights Festival. Each year, Santa and Mrs. Claus visit Cathedral Square Park during this free outdoor event. Kids will have the chance to share their special wishes while parents snap a special keepsake photo. The whole family can enjoy live entertainment, meet the elves and other holiday characters, and indulge in free treats like hot cocoa and cookies.

Pro Tip: If you want to stay for lunch downtown after the event, many restaurants near Cathedral Square Park offer kid-friendly menus and affordable prices just for this occasion.

Christmas Express Santa Train with the East Troy Railroad ($$)

East Troy Depot
2002 Church St.,
East Troy, WI 53120
(262) 642-3263
easttroyrr.org

This magical ride will take you a half hour from the East Troy Depot to Santa's workshop located at the Elegant Farmer. Children can visit Santa and get a photo taken, plus enjoy a craft project and some hot chocolate and cookies. Don't worry, the trolleys are heated and bathrooms are available in the East Troy Depot.

Helpful Hint: Boarding is only done at the East Troy Depot and advance reservations are required. Tickets are non-refundable and non-transferable, and all ticket sales are final.

Soda with Santa at Sprecher Brewery ($)
701 W. Glendale Ave.,
Milwaukee, WI 53209
(414) 964-7837
sprecherbrewery.com
On select Sundays each winter,
Sprecher offers a special event
that includes a family-friendly
brewery tour, a visit and photo
with Santa, a commemorative
glass, beer samples for adults,
gourmet soda samples for kids
of all ages, and personalized root
beer bottle greeting cards.

An Old World Christmas at Old World Wisconsin ($$)
Old World Wisconsin
W372 S9727 Wisconsin 67,
Eagle, WI 53119
(262) 594-6301
oldworldwisconsin.
wisconsinhistory.org

Celebrate Christmas the 19th-
century way at Old World
Wisconsin, featuring storytelling,
live performances by holiday
characters from Wisconsin's
immigrant past, free horse-drawn
bobsled rides (or wagon rides, if
there's no snow on the ground),
caroling and hymn singing, food
sampling from old-fashioned
recipes, photos with Santa Claus,
and more. The 19th-century
crossroads village is trimmed
for the holidays, and wood-fired
stoves and bonfires bring holiday
warmth and good cheer. In past
years, they've even fired up
their Finnish sauna!

Santa's Mailbox in Cathedral Square Park (*)
520 E. Wells St.,
Milwaukee, WI 53202
milwaukeedowntown.com
Kids of all ages can mail their
letters to Santa using this special
mailbox in Cathedral Square
Park. Every child who writes to
Santa will receive a personalized
letter in return. No postage is
necessary, but don't forget to
include your return address.

Makesgiving (*)
Milwaukee Makerspace
2555 S. Lenox St.,
Milwaukee, WI 53207
(262) 490-4531
milwaukeemakerspace.org
Milwaukee Makerspace and
the Bay View Neighborhood
Association present this free
community event every year on
Black Friday. It gives kids and
families the opportunity to learn
new crafty skills and create their
own unique, handcrafted gifts.
Past projects have included DIY
wrapping paper, melted crayon
ornaments, sugar scrubs, and 3D
printer products.

Holiday Floral Show at the Domes ($)

Mitchell Park Horticultural
Conservatory
524 S. Layton Blvd.,
Milwaukee, WI 53215
(414) 257-5611
county.milwaukee.gov

Festive Friday Eves at Cedar Creek Settlement (*)

N70 W6340 Bridge Rd.,
Cedarburg, WI 53012
(262) 377-4763
cedarcreeksettlement.com
On the Friday evenings leading
up to Christmas each year, Cedar
Creek Settlement in Cedarburg
hosts charming events that include
live music, sweet treats, make and
take projects, wine tasting, cookie
decorating, and more.

There is a different theme to the
holiday show each year, but it's
always festive, colorful, and awe-
inspiring. The focal point is the
25 foot holiday tree in the Show
Dome, intricately decorated and
perfect for photo opportunities.

New Year's Eve Celebrations for Kids

New Year's Eve at Noon ($)
Betty Brinn
Children's Museum
929 E. Wisconsin Ave.,
Milwaukee, WI 53202
(414) 390-5437
bbcmkids.org
Each year, Betty Brinn
Children's Museum offers a
family-friendly New Year's Eve
Party that features arts and
crafts activities in the Makers
Space, song and dance, and a
sparkling juice toast at noon.

New Year's Eve at the Domes ($)
524 S. Layton Blvd.,
Milwaukee, WI 53215
(414) 257-5611
milwaukeedomes.org
The Milwaukee Domes hosts a
family-friendly New Year's Eve
party each year, complete with
a DJ Dance Party, face painting,
magician, fire eaters, balloon
twisting, arts and crafts, party
favors for the kids, and a light
show and balloon drop in the
Show Dome. There is a full bar
and food available, as well.

Cool Fool Kite Festival (*)
New Year's Day
Veterans Park
1300 N. Lincoln Memorial Dr.,
Milwaukee, WI 53202
(414) 273-5483
giftofwings.com
This free annual kite festival held
annually on New Year's Day
offers giant kites, free hot cocoa
and coffee, snacks, ice artists,
ice carving lessons, and hot food
for purchase. You can bring your
own kite to fly or purchase one
at Gift of Wings.

Martin Luther King Jr. Day

Dr. Martin Luther King Jr. annual birthday celebration

January
Marcus Center for the
Performing Arts
929 N. Water St.,
Milwaukee, WI 53202
(414) 273-7121
marcuscenter.org
Every year in January, the Marcus Center for the Performing Arts keeps Dr. King's legacy alive with a birthday celebration that highlights young people in the community through art, speech, and writing. There is always live entertainment with cultural arts organizations from around the city.

Martin Luther King Library Annual Celebration

January
310 W. Locust St.,
Milwaukee, WI 53212
(414) 286-3000
mpl.org
Each year, the Martin Luther King Library hosts a celebration on Martin Luther King Day that includes hands-on activities for kids, visits from dignitaries, and live entertainment throughout the day. The library also houses a collection of permanent art, some of it having to do with Dr. Martin Luther King Jr.

Don't miss it! Look for Amos Paul Kennedy Jr.'s accordion book, which showcases Dr. King's most famous quotations.

Did you know? The only cities that have celebrated Dr. King's birthday annually since 1984 are Atlanta, Georgia and Milwaukee, Wisconsin.

Sleigh & Dog-Sled Rides

Horse-drawn Sleigh Rides at Apple Holler ($$)
5006 S. Sylvania Ave.,
Sturtevant, WI 53177
(262) 884-7100
appleholler.com
The old-fashioned sleigh rides at Apple Holler take you and your family through the snow-covered orchards and 100-year-old hardwoods, while you enjoy the scenery and listen to the clopping of the Amish Haflinger horses pulling you. Afterwards, you'll enjoy s'mores around a campfire and a cup of hot cocoa or warm apple cider.

Dog Sled Rides with Door County Sled Dogs ($$)
(414) 967-9677
doorcountysleddogs.com
This non-profit organization is run entirely by volunteers, and their sled team is made up of lovable rescued dogs. They race for charities and offer dog sled rides in Whitnall Park. Rides are usually offered January through February, but they are weather dependent. You'll get to visit with the dogs, ask questions of their humans, take pictures, and enjoy a dog sled ride on the trail. There is a warming house with concessions and a sledding hill nearby. Check the website or call the Sled Dog Hotline for the most updated details.

Horse-drawn Sleigh Rides at Paradise Ranch ($$$)
2408 Spring Hill Dr.,
Cedarburg, WI 53012
(262) 825-7500
paradiseranchwi.com
The sleigh rides at Paradise Ranch are pulled by majestic Percheron horses that take you through forty acres of woods decorated with twinkling Christmas lights. The sleigh holds up to 12 people. Afterwards, you can sit around the campfire with s'mores, or enjoy the heated, festive barn and a warm drink.

Ice Skating

Top picks:

Lake Park (*)
2975 N. Lake Park Rd.,
Milwaukee, WI 53211
(414) 962-1680
lakeparkfriends.org
Head to this picturesque gem overlooking Lake Michigan for public skating during the winter months. While you're there, you can also stop by the North Point Lighthouse or play on the playground.

Did you know? Lake Park has something in common with Central Park in New York City and the U.S. Capitol Grounds in Washington D.C. All three were designed by the same landscape architect, Frederick Law Olmsted.

Red Arrow Park (*)
920 N. Water St.,
Milwaukee, WI 53202
(414) 289-8791
county.milwaukee.gov
You can visit this downtown landmark January through March for free ice skating (with skate rentals available at a small cost). Remodeled in 1999, the ice rink can fit around 100 people at a time and is conveniently located right next to a Starbucks, so you can enjoy a hot chocolate or coffee if you need to warm up.

Fun fact: The 128 by 95 foot ice rink in Red Arrow Park is actually bigger than the one at Rockefeller Center.

Helpful hint: Ice sleds are available for people with mobility limitations.

Pettit National Ice Center ($) 🎂 🔥
500 S. 84th St.,
Milwaukee, WI 53214
(414) 266-0100
thepettit.com
The Pettit National Ice Center is a 200,000 square foot indoor ice skating facility in Milwaukee, Wisconsin, featuring two international-size ice rinks and a 400-meter speed skating oval. Public skating times, rental skate fees, and occasional promotions are listed on their website. They also offer ice skating classes for all ages throughout the year. (Don't forget to bring a coat! It may be an indoor facility, but it is still chilly.)

Burnham Playfield (*)

1755 S. 32nd St.,
Milwaukee, WI 53215
(414) 647-6046

This free community ice rink is operated by the Milwaukee Recreation Department and the Epic Center Community Organization. They provide open skating opportunities, free skate rentals, and a warning house with hot cocoa for sale. There is also pond hockey on designated evenings.

Humboldt Park Lagoon (*)

3000 S. Howell Ave.,
Milwaukee, WI 53207
(414) 257-8005
humboldtparkmilwaukee.org

If you're looking for an outdoor ice skating experience, head to the Humboldt Park lagoon. The lagoon is surrounded by a majestic park, and it's a lovely way to spend a winter afternoon. Check first for updated hours and lagoon conditions on the Humboldt Park Friends website. There are convenient bathrooms located right across the street from the lagoon in the Pavilion.

Lynden Sculpture Garden ($)

2145 W. Brown Deer Rd.,
Milwaukee, WI 53217
(414) 446-8794
lyndensculpturegarden.org

View unique sculptures from the middle of the lake. Bring your own skates! Regular garden admission rates will apply.

Scout Lake (*)

5902 W. Loomis Rd.,
Greendale, WI 53129
(414) 425-7303
county.milwaukee.gov

Check the Milwaukee County website for public skate and warming house hours to ice skate on this beautiful five acre lake.

Sheridan Park (*)

4800 S. Lake Dr.,
Cudahy, WI 53110
(414) 762-1550

Enjoy the stunning view of the downtown skyline from Sheridan Park. This ice rink is lit for nighttime ice skating, but there is no warming house.

Urban Ecology Center at Washington Park (*)

1859 N. 40th St.,
Milwaukee, WI 53208
(414) 344-5460
urbanecologycenter.org

Skate outdoors at the lagoon, then warm up with some hot chocolate at the Urban Ecology Center in Washington Park. Check their website for public hours and conditions. The lagoon isn't usually ready for skating until January or February.

Wilson Ice Arena ($) 🎂 🔥

4001 S. 20th St.,
Milwaukee, WI 53221
(414) 281-6289
county.milwaukee.gov

Skate all year round on their National Hockey League sized rink (200 by 85 feet). There are also locker rooms, a concession area, and rental skates.

Milwaukee County

Fox Point Ice Rink / Longacre Skating Pavilion (*)
7343 N. Longacre Rd.,
Milwaukee, WI 53217
village.fox-point.wi.us

Hart Park (*)
7201 W. State St.,
Wauwatosa, WI 53213
wauwatosa.net

LaFollette Park (*)
9418 W. Washington St.,
Milwaukee, WI 53214
(414) 587-8217
friendsoflafollettepark.com

McCarty Park (*)
8214 W. Cleveland Ave.,
West Allis, WI 53219
(414) 672-5052
county.milwaukee.gov

Ozaukee County

Festive Ice Rink (*)
Cedar Creek Park
N55 W6079 Portland Rd.,
Cedarburg, WI 53012
ci.cedarburg.wi.us

Homestead Hollow County Park (*)
N120 W19809 Freistadt Rd.,
Germantown, WI 53022
(262) 335-4445
co.washington.wi.us

Kinderberg Park (*)
N106W15060 Buckthorn Dr.,
Germantown, WI 53022
(262) 250-4700
village.germantown.wi.us

Mee-Kwon Park (*)
6333 W. Boniwell Rd.,
Mequon, WI 53097
(262) 242-1310
co.ozaukee.wi.us

Ozaukee Ice Center ($) 🎂 🔥
5505 Pioneer Rd. # 144N,
Mequon, WI 53097
(262) 375-6851
ozaukeeicecenter.org

Washington County

Firemen's Park (*)
645 Baehring Dr.,
Slinger, WI 53086
(262) 644-5265
vi.slinger.wi.gov

Regner Park (*)
800 N. Main St.,
West Bend, WI 53090
(262) 335-5100
ci.west-bend.wi.us

Ridge Run Park
300 S. University Dr.,
West Bend, WI 53095
(262) 338-1012
ci.west-bend.wi.us

Waukesha County

Eble Ice Arena ($) 🏠 ♨
19400 W. Bluemound Rd.,
Brookfield, WI 53045
(262) 784-5155
waukeshacounty.gov/
ebleicearena

Malone Park (*) - *Illuminated*
16400 W. Al Stigler Pkwy.,
New Berlin, WI 53151
(262) 786-8610
newberlin.org

Nagawaukee Park Ice Arena (*) 🏠
2699 Golf Rd.,
Delafield, WI 53018
(262) 646-7072
waukeshacounty.gov/
nagawaukeeicearena

The Ponds of Brookfield ($) 🏠 ♨
2810 N. Calhoun Rd.,
Brookfield, WI 53005
(262) 786-7663
thepondsofbrookfield.com
Check their website for specific Open Skate hours, skate rental fees, or to find out more about their Learn to Skate program.

Skiing, Snowboarding & Tubing

Wilmot Mountain ($$$)
11931 Fox River Rd.,
Wilmot, WI 53192
(262) 862-2301
wilmotmountain.com
Wilmot Mountain has been a snow sport destination for Wisconsinites since 1938. Today you can ski, snowboard or tube over 120 acres, 23 ski trails, and 22 tube lanes. Much of the property has been recently redesigned and modernized, including their base lodge which offers wi-fi, "Walt's Tavern" restaurant where parents can watch their children ski and snowboard, and a state-of-the-art children's ski and snowboard center featuring a playful open space for kids.

Alpine Valley Resort ($$$)

W2501 County Road D,
Elkhorn, WI 53121
(262) 642-7374
alpinevalleyresort.com
Alpine Valley Resort is set in the
rolling terrain of the Sugar Creek
Valley, and offers over 90 acres
and 20 ski runs. It is the only
resort in southeastern Wisconsin
that features on site ski-in and
ski-out rooms. With a full service
dining bistro and free weekend
family movie nights, it lends itself
to a fun weekend getaway

If you're new to the sport, head
to the spacious and enclosed
beginner area with gentle slopes,
perfect for kids. You can even
hop on the Wonder Carpet lifts,
moving conveyor belts that help
beginners easily stand and ride to
the top of the beginner hill.

There is also a scenic, tree-lined
trail for intermediate skiers that
consists of 1400 feet of natural
rolling landscape fully lined with
mature trees.

Lessons are available for ages
five and up, and take place in the
Terrain Based Learning Area.

Fun Fact: The steepest run
is Big Thunder and the longest
slope is Alpine.

Little Switzerland ($$$)

105 Cedar Creek Rd.,
Slinger, WI 53086
(262) 297-9621
littleswitz.com
Just a short ride from downtown
Milwaukee, Little Switzerland
offers a beginners area, two
easy runs, eight difficult trails,
and freestyle terrain. They offer
private lessons for kids six and
under, and general lessons for
ages seven and up. Warm up,
grab a cup of soup, and watch
the action from The Chalet, a
historic lodge on site.

Sunburst Winter Sports Park ($$$)

8355 Prospect Dr.,
Kewaskum, WI 53040
(262) 626-8404
skisunburst.com
Just 30 minutes northwest of
Milwaukee, Sunburst offers
skiing, snowboarding, and tubing
in three terrain parks. Their claim
to fame is that it is the world's
largest tubing park with over 45
lanes. It was even recognized
by USA Today as one of the top
ten tubing parks in the entire
country.

After a long day on the slopes,
you'll appreciate their fresh
food cafe serving up artisan
sandwiches and salads, plus
Starbuck's coffee and espresso
drinks to help you warm up.

The Mountaintop at Grand Geneva ($$$)
7036 Grand Geneva Way,
Lake Geneva, WI 53147
(800) 558-3417
grandgeneva.com

The Mountaintop at Grand Geneva offers more than 30 acres of ski runs for a variety of abilities. Their snowmaking capabilities ensure that you can ski regardless of the weather. Lessons are available for kids and adults. When you're not skiing you can relax in the Mountain Top Lodge. Kids six and under ski free with an adult.

The Rock Snowpark ($$$)
7900B W Crystal Ridge Rd.,
Franklin, WI 53132
(414) 235-8818
rocksnowpark.com

The Rock Snowpark is located just outside of the city of Milwaukee, and your season passes here will also be valid at Little Switzerland. It's the most affordable option featured here. Besides skiing and snowboarding, all ages can enjoy riding the conveyor lift and tubing down one of the many snow chutes.

Snowshoeing

If you can walk, you can snowshoe.

Snowshoeing gives you the opportunity to enjoy a Wisconsin winter in a whole new way. The following nature centers offer snowshoe rentals and kid-friendly trails.

Havenwoods State Forest (*)
6141 N. Hopkins St.,
Milwaukee, WI 53209
(414) 527-0232
dnr.wi.gov/topic/parks/name/havenwoods

Snowshoers are welcome to explore over 6 miles of trails in Havenwoods State Forest, and you can borrow snowshoes any time the nature center is open. The "People and the Land" trail is especially kid friendly at just 1.3 miles.

Wehr Nature Center ($)

9701 W College Ave.,
Franklin, WI 53132
(414) 425-8550
friendsofwehr.org

Anyone over five years old can
rent snowshoes for up to three
hours between 9:00 a.m. and 4:00
p.m. for $10/pair. You can use
them throughout Whitnall Park.

Urban Ecology Center

Riverside Park:
1500 E. Park Pl.,
Milwaukee, WI 53211
(414) 964-8505
Washington Park:
1859 N. 40th St.,
Milwaukee, WI 53208
(414) 344-5460
Menomonee Valley:
3700 W. Pierce St.,
Milwaukee, WI 53215
(414) 431-2940
urbanecologycenter.org

By becoming a member at the
Urban Ecology Center, you'll
have the opportunity to rent
out their nature equipment,
including snowshoes.

Schlitz Audubon Nature Center ($)

1111 E. Brown Deer Rd.,
Milwaukee, WI 53217
(414) 352-2880
schlitzaudubon.org

Keep an eye on the Schlitz
Audubon Nature Center website
and calendar. They occasionally
offer low-cost, guided Family
Snowshoe events, during which
they provide the snowshoes.

Hawthorn Glen ($)

1130 N 60th St.,
Milwaukee, WI 53208
(414) 647-6050
milwaukeerecreation.net

Keep an eye on the Hawthorn
Glen Facebook Page. They
occasionally offer low-cost
snowshoe hikes for which they
provide snowshoes. Sometimes
the hikes are even candlelit!

Sledding/Tobogganing

Any old hill will do, of course, but here are some of the most well-known places to go sledding around Milwaukee:

Top pick: Whitnall Park (*)
5879 S. 92nd St.,
Franklin, WI 53132
countyparks.com
Located near the Boerner Botanical Gardens, this 400 foot sledding hill is free to the public, lit up at night, and features a toboggan run. There is also a smaller hill for the little ones north of the main hill. There is ample parking in the large lot off of 92nd street, and you can enjoy warm concessions in the Whitnall Clubhouse.

Don't miss it! *Don't miss your chance to ride with the Door County Sled Dogs, a recreational dog sled team made up of rescued dogs and run by an all volunteer organization. Sled rides are typically offered in Whitnall Park on the weekends for all ages on a first come, first served basis. You'll get to visit with the dogs, ask questions, take pictures, and ride with the dogs around the trail. The cost starts around $15, and you can call (414) 967-9677 for the most up-to-date information.*

Top pick: Lowell Park Toboggan Run ($) 🧁
Lowell Park Warming Shelter
2201 Michigan Ave.,
Waukesha, WI 53188
For updated conditions and hours, call (262) 522-9356
waukesha-wi.gov
Located near Lowell Elementary School, the park offers great sledding and a 350 foot lighted toboggan run. Sleds are also available to rent. You must sign a waiver, which are available at the shelter, and all riders must be 48 inches or taller. Children under 11 must ride with an adult.

Milwaukee County (*)
*Starred parks are lit up at night from 4:30 p.m. - 8:30 p.m.! Get the most updated information by visiting countyparks.com.

Brown Deer Park
7835 N. Green Bay Ave.,
Milwaukee, WI 53209
Short hill with steep drop.

Columbus Park
7301 W. Courtland Ave.,
Milwaukee, WI 53218

*Currie Park
3535 N. Mayfair Rd.,
Wauwatosa, WI 53222
This golf course converts into a long, shallow sledding hill in the winter. The moderate speed is good for all ages. Warm up and grab a snack in the Currie Park Golf Dome nearby.

Greene Park
4235 S. Lipton Ave.,
St. Francis, WI 53235

Hales Corners Park
5765 S. New Berlin Rd.,
Hales Corners, WI 53130

*Humboldt Park
3000 S. Howell Ave.,
Milwaukee, WI 53207

LaFollette Park
9418 W. Washington St.,
Milwaukee, WI 53214
Not steep; slow speed

McCarty Park
8214 W. Cleveland Ave.,
West Allis, WI 53219

McGovern Park
5400 N. 51st Blvd.,
Milwaukee, WI 53218

*Pulaski Park
1644-1712 W. Cleveland Ave.,
Milwaukee, WI 53215

Wilson Park
1601 W. Howard Ave.,
Milwaukee, WI 53221

More in Milwaukee County:

Bayside Village Hall (*)
9075 N. Regent Rd.,
Bayside, WI 53217
bayside-wi.gov
You'll find the Village of Bayside's sledding hill just north of Village Hall on the corner of Fairy Chasm Road and Regent Road. Parking is available on the west side of the sledding hill or in the Village Hall South Parking Lot.

Chapel Hills Park (*)
6735 S. Highfield Dr.,
Oak Creek, WI 53154
(414) 768-6515

Hart Park (*)
7201 W. State St.,
Wauwatosa, WI 53213
Wauwatosa.net

Honey Creek Sled Hill / Dewey Hill (*)
7620-7624 N. Honey Creek Pkwy.,
Wauwatosa, WI 53213
Located in a county park, this hill is open to the public and it's rather steep. The west side of the slope is safer for young kids.

Kletzsch Park (*)
6560 N. Milwaukee River Pkwy., Glendale, WI 53209
kletszchfriends.org

Manor Marquette Park (*)
E. Marquette Ave.,
Oak Creek, WI 53154
(414) 768-6568

Riverton Meadows Park (*)
2800 E. Honeysuckle Dr.,
Oak Creek, WI 53154
(414) 257-7275

Urban Ecology Center (*)
Riverside Park:
1500 E. Park Pl.,
Milwaukee, WI 53211
(414) 964-8505
Washington Park:
1859 N. 40th St.,
Milwaukee, WI 53208
(414) 344-5460
Menomonee Valley:
3700 W. Pierce St.,
Milwaukee, WI 53215
(414) 431-2940
urbanecologycenter.org
All three branches offer sledding adventures, free rentals for members, and hot cocoa and tea inside.

Ozaukee County

Behling Field (*)
N52W5882 Portland Rd.,
Cedarburg, WI 53012
(262) 375-7600
ci.cedarburg.wi.us

Centennial Park (*)
W68 N851 Evergreen Blvd.,
Cedarburg, WI 53012
(262) 375-7600
ci.cedarburg.wi.us

Fisher Park (*)
N70 W6110 Bridge Rd.,
Cedarburg, WI 53012
(262) 375-7600
ci.cedarburg.wi.us

Mee-Kwon Park (*)
6333 W. Boniwell Rd.,
Mequon, WI 53097
co.ozaukee.wi.us
Locally known as "Mule Hill", Mee-Kwon Park is home to a sledding hill with a long shallow grade. There is ice skating at the nearby pond, as well, where you'll find a warming house. There is no skating or sledding allowed at night.

Lime Kiln Park (*)
2020 S. Green Bay Rd.,
Grafton, WI 53024
After sledding, check out the historic lime kilns.

Legion Memorial Park (*)
W57N481 Hilbert Ave.,
Cedarburg, WI 53012
ci.cedarburg.wi.us
You'll find the sledding hill off Spring St. in the back of the park.

Hawthorn Hills Park (*)
4720 County Rd. I,
Saukville, WI 53080
This popular golf course converts into a sledding hill for all ages during the winter months.

Washington County

Kinderberg Park (*)
N106W15060 Buckthorn Dr.,
Germantown, WI 53022
(262) 250-4710
village.germantown.wi.us

Homestead Hollow County Park (*)
N120 W19809 Freistadt Rd.,
Germantown, WI 53022
(262) 335-4445
co.washington.wi.us

Erin Go Bragh Park (*)
1846 WI-83,
Hartford, WI 53027
erintownship.com

Lisbon Community Park (*)
N78 W26970 Bartlett Pkwy.,
Lisbon, WI
(262) 246-7266
townoflisbonwi.com

Firemen's Park (*)
645 Baehring Dr.,
Slinger, WI 53086
(262) 644-5265
vi.slinger.wi.gov

*Ridge Run Park (*)
300 S. University Dr.,
West Bend, WI 53095
(262) 338-1012
ci.west-bend.wi.us

Royal Oaks Park (*)
1000 Auburn Rd.,
West Bend, WI 53090
(262) 335-5100
ci.west-bend.wi.us

Waukesha County

Park Arthur (*)
S63W17833 College Ave.,
Muskego, WI 53150
(262) 679-4108
cityofmuskego.org

Calhoun Park (*)
5400 S. Calhoun Rd.,
New Berlin, WI 53151
newberlin.org

Elm Grove Village Park (*)
13600 Juneau Blvd.,
Elm Grove, WI 53122
(262) 782-6700
elmgrovewi.org

Fowler Park (*)
438 N. Oakwood Ave.,
Oconomowoc, WI 53066
(262) 569-2199
oconomowoc-wi.gov

Gatewood Park (*)
14201 W. Kostner Ln.,
New Berlin, WI 53151
(262) 786-8610
newberlin.org

Genesee Lake Road Park (*)
37505 Genesee Lake Rd.,
Summit, WI 53066
(262) 567-2757
summitvillage.org

"Killer Hill" (*)
MacArthur Ave. (between
Menomonee and Norman)
Menomonee Falls, WI 53051

Menomonee Park (*)
W220 N7884 Town Line Rd.,
Menomonee Falls, WI 53051
(262) 255-1310
waukeshacounty.gov

Minooka Park (*)
1927 E. Sunset Dr.,
Waukesha, WI 53189
(262) 896-8006
waukeshacounty.gov

Mitchell Park (*)
19900 River Rd.,
Brookfield, WI 53045
(262) 782-9650
ci.brookfield.wi.us

Mukwonago Park (*)
S100W31900 County Hwy
LO, Mukwonago, WI 53149
(262) 548-7801
waukeshacounty.gov

Nashotah Park (*)
W330n5113 County Rd. C,
Nashotah, WI 53058
(262) 367-1022
waukeshacounty.gov

Lauren Park (*)
W315S8555 County Rd. EE
Mukwonago, WI 53149

Liberty Park (*)
440 Concord Rd.,
Pewaukee, Wisconsin 53072

Nature Hill (*)
850 Lake Dr.,
Oconomowoc, WI 53066

Sussex Village Park (*)
N64W23760 Main St.,
Sussex, WI 53089
(262) 246-5200
villagesussex.org

*Valley View Park (*)
5051 S. Sunny Slope Rd., New
Berlin, WI 53151
(262) 797-2443
newberlin.org

Wales Community Park (*)
420 W. Brandybrook Rd.,
Wales, WI 53183

**Wirth Park/
Wirth Park South (*)**
2585 Pilgrim Rd.,
Brookfield, WI 53005
(262) 787-3901
ci.brookfield.wi.us

Ice Fishing

Milwaukee County Parks (*)

(414) 257-7275
county.milwaukee.gov/parks
Each year, Milwaukee County Parks and Waukesha County Parks offer free fishing clinics for kids 15 years and younger in parks throughout the city. In most cases, clinics are held at park lagoons. The clinics are taught by members of local fishing clubs and include fishing instruction, safety knot tying, and how to properly use equipment. Small children must be accompanied by an adult. Fishing equipment is available, but you can bring your own rod and reel if you have them.

Annual Winter Festivals

Cool Fool Kite Festival (*)

January
Veterans Park
1300 N. Lincoln Memorial Dr., Milwaukee, WI 53202
(414) 273-5483
giftofwings.com
This free, annual kite festival held on New Year's Day offers free hot cocoa and coffee, snacks, giant kites, ice artists, ice carving lessons, and hot food for purchase. You can bring your own kite to fly or purchase one at Gift of Wings.

Love Your Great Lakes Day ($$)

Discovery World
500 N Harbor Dr., Milwaukee, WI 53202
(414) 765-8634
discoveryworld.org
Love Your Great Lakes Day is an annual family-friendly event at Discovery World that celebrates the Great Lakes with hands-on and interactive activities. It's packed with local organizations that are committed to sustaining the Great Lakes.

Waukesha Janboree (*)
January
janboree.org
Get it? "January" and "Jamboree" are combined to create "Janboree!" This epic event opens with a special ceremony that includes a dance, live music, and fireworks outside on the Fox River. Activities throughout the weekend include ice sculpting demonstrations, a pancake breakfast, trolley rides, ice bocce ball, indoor ice skating at Eble Arena, ice fishing clinics, horse-drawn wagon rides, stargazing planetarium shows, nature activities, and more!

Winterfest at the Boerner Botanical Gardens (*)
January
9400 Boerner Dr.,
Hales Corners, WI 53130
(414) 525-5600
boernerbotanicalgardens.org
This free event held in the Boerner Visitor Center offers special nature walks, indoor and outdoor games and activities, hot drinks, and family fun!

Winterfest at the Urban Ecology Center (*)
January
Washington Park
1859 N. 40th St.,
Milwaukee, WI 53208
urbanecologycenter.org
Make the most of winter at this free family festival that celebrates the snow and ice. Take advantage of the Urban Ecology Center's skating rink and sledding hill, and enjoy music, crafts, homemade pies, guided nature walks, and plenty of hot cocoa.

Pro Tip: The Urban Ecology Center also hosts a special "Winterfest for afternoon nappers" in the morning for very young kids.

Winter Carnival at the Lynden Sculpture Garden ($)
2145 W. Brown Deer Rd.,
Milwaukee, WI 53217
lyndensculpturegarden.org
The Lynden Sculpture Garden's annual Winter Carnival features outdoor art-making, studio activities, scavenger hunts, hikes, parades, ice skating, painting the pond, cross-country skiing, snowshoeing, and local artists who showcase projects and performances for all to enjoy.

Winter Frolic at the Mequon Nature Preserve (*)

February

8200 W. County Line Rd., Mequon, WI 53097

mequonnaturepreserve.org

Head to the Mequon Nature Preserve for a free festival that typically includes dog sled demonstrations, tractor rides, live music, a petting zoo, sleigh rides, kid's crafts, ice fishing, bonfires, snowman building, and more.

Winter Festival in Cedarburg (*)

February

Historic Downtown Cedarburg

cedarburgfestival.org

Cedarburg is magical in the winter, and outdoor fun abounds at their Winter Festival. Delight in themed costumed bed races, ice carving competitions, parades, barrel rolling, sledding, ice skating, and even camel rides. Warm up inside, where you'll smell the chili cooking and enjoy live music.

Milwaukee Winter Farmer's Market

Milwaukee Winter Farmer's Market (*)

Saturdays from 9:00 a.m. - 1:00 p.m.

mcwfm.org

The local fresh food supply doesn't stop in the winter. Known for seven years as the "Milwaukee County Winter Farmer's Market" and operated by the Fondy Food Center, this farmer's market offers free parking and admission. You'll find high quality produce along with freshly baked goods, jams, cider, honey, maple syrup, sorghum, sauces and soups, and global cuisine.

Tea Time

The Pfister Hotel ($$$)
424 E. Wisconsin Ave.,
Milwaukee, WI 53202
(414) 273-8222
thepfisterhotel.com

Families can once again enjoy a fancy day out together, inspired by 19th century traditional English teatime at the Pfister Hotel October through April.

Teatime takes place in luxurious Blu on the 23rd floor of the hotel, with sprawling, panoramic views of Milwaukee and Lake Michigan.

Guests can learn about each variety of tea, including its origins, unique flavors, and even its effects on mood and health. You'll enjoy a table side tea blending and all silver service by a Pfister Tea Butler, who makes sure each cup of tea is brewed to perfection. They'll even use a fancy replica of an 18th century self-tipping teapot.

The whole experience is accompanied by delightful live piano music and a cozy fireplace.

The Pfister offers a selection of Rishi Teas in 12 varieties, including its signature blend, Pfister 1893, exclusively crafted in 2013 in conjunction with Milwaukee-based Rishi Tea. Pfister 1893 features a blend of jasmine and wild-rose scented white teas infused with rejuvenating peppermint and calming lavender. Tea is paired with a special menu complete with fresh scones, sandwiches and pastries.

For ladies and gentlemen twelve years and younger, an "All Grown Up" menu is available featuring warm sipping chocolate, lemonade, cider, Vermont ham & cheddar finger sandwiches, herbed chicken salad tartlets, traditional scones and chocolate ganache tartlets.

Did you know? Afternoon tea originated in England in the 1800s, and was often served in the drawing room between four and five o'clock. Women would wear long gowns and men donned their finest suits while they socialized over savory delicacies and sweet treats.

Milwaukee Ballet's Nutcracker Tea ($$$)

The Wisconsin Club's
City Club
900 W. Wisconsin Ave.,
Milwaukee, WI 53233
milwaukeeballet.org

Each year, the Milwaukee Ballet puts on a special tea time event for children ages 3-10 and their parents. It's filled with magical performances, holiday themed crafts, a dance lesson from the Milwaukee Ballet dancers, and a delicious holiday brunch.

Spring

Maple Sugaring

In late February and March, the snow begins to melt, the earliest signs of spring begin to show, and the maple trees are finally ready to be tapped. It's also when local nature centers gear up for their annual maple sugaring events, enabling kids and families to learn about the process in a hands-on, interactive way. It's the perfect time to explore nature with your kids, and learn together about how we turn nature into products that we love. Here are some annual events to check out:

Riveredge Nature Center ($$)

4458 County Hwy Y, Saukville, WI 53080
(262) 375-2715
riveredgenaturecenter.org
Riveredge has over 40 years of experience maple sugaring, and they tap around 400 trees a year. Help prepare for the sugarin' season by tapping the maple trees in Riveredge's sugar bush. You can help drill the holes, tap in the spiles and hang the buckets.

They also put on a Maple Sugarin' Festival with live demonstrations, hands-on activities, music, and more. You can watch the evaporator in action, as the sap is transformed into syrup, and enjoy pancakes with 100% pure Riveredge maple syrup.

Urban Ecology Center ($)

Riverside Park
1500 E. Park Pl., Milwaukee, WI 53211
(414) 964-8505
urbanecologycenter.org
See maple sap harvesting up close in Riverside Park, and eat pancakes afterwards with homemade maple syrup.

Schlitz Audubon Nature Center ($$)

1111 E. Brown Deer Rd.,
Milwaukee, WI 53217
(414) 352-2880
schlitzaudubon.org

The Schlitz Audubon Nature Center hosts a maple sugaring event each year that takes participants through the stages of making maple syrup, including tapping the trees and boiling the sap with the sugar farmer at an evaporator. You also get to try pancakes with maple syrup, of course. Be on the lookout for special "Hand-in-hand" Maple Sugaring events for toddlers and preschoolers, too.

Maple Syrup Family Day (*)

Richfield Nature/
Historical Park
1896 State Road 164,
Richfield, WI 53076
(262) 628-7707
richfieldhistoricalsociety.org

This free event enables families to learn together about the maple syrup process, and see all of the steps up close. There are also demonstrations, story time in the log cabin, tours of historic buildings, wagon rides, and hot food and treats for sale.

Maple Sugar Days at Wehr Nature Center ($)

9701 W. College Ave.,
Franklin, WI 53132
(414) 425-8550
friendsofwehr.org

This annual event at Wehr Nature Center celebrates spring and Wisconsin heritage. Participants get to enjoy a guided hike to an old-fashioned sugarin' camp, see a boil down demonstration up-close, and have access to all kind of hands-on activities. They also sell maple sugar treats and tapping equipment at this festival.

milwaukee
WITH KIDS

St. Patrick's Day

St. Patrick's Day Parade
Downtown Milwaukee
stpatricksparade.org
Hear the bagpipes at the annual St. Patrick's Day Parade featuring Irish dancers, marching bands, Celtic community groups, themed floats, and much more. The parade typically begins at noon at 3rd Street and Wisconsin Avenue, and finishes at the corner of Water Street and Highland Avenue.

Annual Easter Celebrations

Bunny Train
East Troy Electric Railroad
2002 Church St.,
East Troy, WI 53120
(262) 642-3263
easttroyrr.org
Start your adventures at the East Troy depot with kids activities like face painting. Then enjoy Easter-themed activities aboard a ten-mile round trip to the Elegant Farmer, where you'll get to see live bunnies and chicks on display by local 4-H students. Visit with the Easter Bunny for pictures and enjoy a treat before returning to East Troy on board the full size train. The historic railroad cars are heated and restrooms are available at the depot.

Cheep Cheep Easter Celebration at Elegant Farmer (*)
1545 Main St.,
Mukwonago, WI 53149
(262) 363-6770
elegantfarmer.com
Head out to the country for this free, family-fun event that

features the Easter Bunny, a 4-H menagerie of bunnies in costume, baby chicks, and guinea pigs for petting. 4-H members will be on hand to educate and introduce children of all ages to the animals they have raised and cared for as part of their 4-H project. Easter specialty foods are always available this time of year, including cider baked ham, fresh breads, and Easter basket candies.

Egg Day at the Zoo ($$)

Milwaukee County Zoo
10001 W Bluemound Rd.,
Milwaukee, WI 53226
(414) 771-3040
milwaukeezoo.org
Highlights of this special Easter event at the zoo include a bright-colored egg hunt, an Easter Parade, face painting, DIY bunny ears, animal enrichment activities, expert "bubbleologists," and more.

Easter at Boerner Botanical Gardens (*)

9400 Boerner Dr.,
Hales Corners, WI 53130
(414) 525-5600
boernerbotanicalgardens.org
Meet the Easter Bunny and join the Friends of Boerner Botanical Gardens for Easter crafts and an egg hunt. You can also enjoy a delicious Easter Brunch with Zilli Hospitality Group (brunch not included in FBBG event).

Kid-Friendly Art Centers

Latino Arts, Inc. ($)

1028 S. 9th St.,
Milwaukee, WI 53204
(414) 384-3100
latinoartsinc.org

Start your day at the Latino Art Center by exploring their intimate and kid-friendly gallery that showcases Hispanic artists from all over. Next to the gallery is a performance space where the center welcomes Latino musical artists from all over the world. Just outside the gallery is the community's Hispanic Heritage Center, which provides an opportunity to browse their small exhibits and talk with your kids about the contributions of Latinos to the local community. You can also browse handmade goods that help support the mission of the Latino Arts Center. End your visit with a bite to eat at the Cafe el Sol.

Helpful hints:
-Download the self-guided walking tour from their website to make sure you see all of the bright, colorful murals in the heart of the Latin Quarter.

-Visit the gallery during the month of October leading up to Día de los Muertos (Day of the Dead), when you'll find authentic altars honoring loved ones who have passed.

Schauer Arts & Activities Center ($$)

147 N. Rural St.,
Hartford, WI 53027
(262) 670-0560
schauercenter.org

The Schauer Community School of the Arts offers year-round classes in dance, music, theater, and visual arts, for students of all ages and levels.

Sharon Lynne Wilson Center for the Arts ($$) 🧁

19805 W. Capitol Dr.,
Brookfield, WI 53045
(262) 781-9470
wilson-center.com

Nestled in Mitchell Park in Brookfield, the Wilson Center greets its visitors with a modern, illuminated sculpture. Your kids will love to pose for a picture in front of it! You and your children can take classes like watercolor painting and film animation, or you can host an art-themed birthday party at their updated facility.

In the Art of Nature Camp at the Wilson Center, kids can explore the natural world through the arts. Teaching artists help campers discover the sounds, patterns, colors, and rhythms in the surrounding park.

Don't miss it!
-The Wilson Center hosts a family-friendly concert series called Starry Nights in the summer on Friday nights.

Walker's Point Center for the Arts (*) 🏠 🔥

839 S. 5th St.,
Milwaukee, WI 53204
(414) 672-2787
wpca-milwaukee.org
Walker's Point Center for the Arts is a community arts center dedicated to supporting the arts in a multicultural environment. You can visit their gallery or participate in one of their kid-friendly programs. They have organized an extensive and affordable educational program for Milwaukee area youth ages 6-12. They conclude each summer with an annual gallery showing of student work.

The WPCA's educational art programs include:
• Afternoons with Art on MPS non-school days
• Free after school art classes during the academic year
• Summer Art Camps in the summer

Waukesha Community Arts Project (*)

320 South St.,
Waukesha, WI 53186
(262) 480-5482
wcartproject.net
The Waukesha Community Arts Project (WCAP) provides free, after-school art classes in visual arts, drama, dance and creative writing for middle-school students five days a week during the school year.

Art Museums

Haggerty Museum of Art (*)

530 N. 13th St.,
Milwaukee, WI 53233
(414) 288-1669
marquette.edu/haggerty/
The Haggerty Museum of Art is tucked away on the Marquette Campus, on the corner of 13th Street and Clybourne Avenue. It features eight to nine exciting exhibits every year, and it's completely free for visitors.

Pro tip: You can park in Marquette University's Lot J, accessed from North 11th Street between Wisconsin Avenue and Clybourn Street. There are 15 spaces in the lot dedicated just to Haggerty guests. More parking is available in the Wells Street Parking Structure, or at metered spaces on Clybourn Avenue.

Lynden Sculpture Garden ($$) 🏠 🔥

2145 W. Brown Deer Rd.,
Milwaukee, WI 53217
(414) 446-8794
lyndensculpturegarden.org

The must-visit Lynden Sculpture Garden offers a unique experience of art in nature through its collection of more than 50 monumental sculptures across 40 acres of park, lake and woodland. They offer a monthly Tuesday in the Garden program for small children and weekly art drop-in programs for older kids. (These programs fill up fast, so you must pre-register.)

Lynden's art and nature camps for children aged 20 months to 15 years integrate their collection of monumental outdoor sculpture with the natural ecology of its hidden landscapes and unique habitats. The programs are led by artists, naturalists, and art educators. Past activities have included hatching and raising chickens, building rafts to float across the pond, exploring the mechanics of flight or the physics of flotation, digging in the garden, or pit-firing beads made from local clay.

Helpful hints:
- *During your visit, you can check out a Plein Air kit for outdoor watercolor painting.*
- *Family Kits are available at the front desk and are included with the price of admission. They include a sculpture scavenger hunt, nature activities to complete on the grounds, magnifying glasses, and more.*
- *The grounds provide a perfect spot for a picnic during warm months.*
- *Families can snow-shoe during the winter around the sculpture garden.*
- *Don't miss the whimsical and colorful cow sculpture (actually called Des Vaches: Mo, Ni, Que by Swiss artist Samuel Buri.)*

Milwaukee Art Museum ($$) 🍴

700 Art Museum Dr.,
Milwaukee, WI 53202
(414) 224-3200
mam.org

Did you know that kids under 12 are always admitted for free at the world-class Milwaukee Art Museum? It's also free to everyone on the first Thursday of every month.

Here are some worthwhile things to do with kids at the MAM:

1.) Visit the Kohl's Art Generation Open Studio, open Saturday–Sunday, 10 a.m. to 4 p.m. and 10:00 a.m. - 7:00 p.m. on Thursdays. Kids and families can explore different art materials and techniques used to create the art works in the museum's collection. Themes change monthly, so check their website for updated information.

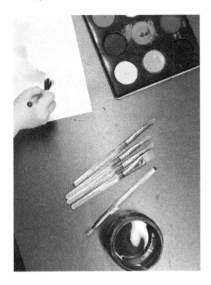

2.) Check out the free Artpacks at the ArtPack Station in Windhover Hall. They are filled with activities that can be used in the galleries each time you visit the museum. They're designed for a wide range of ages and attention spans. Activities include sketch packs, picture books, custom puzzles, puppets, and more.

3.) Take a family audio tour to learn about art through games, videos, and scavenger hunts! Everyone will make surprising connections throughout the galleries while playing art games designed to engage the whole family. You can download the app for free.

4.) Kohl's Art Generation Family Sundays - Five times a year, enjoy hands-on art activities, interactive performances, family tours, visiting artists, and more.

5.) Play Date with Art - This drop-in monthly program is designed for the museum's youngest visitors. Stop and sing along during Singing Time at 10:30 a.m. and 11:15 a.m.

6.) Story Time in the Galleries - Every Saturday at 10:30 a.m., come hear a story that relates to a work of art in the galleries, and then create your own story or drawing to take home.

7.) Take an Art Class for Kids - The Museum offers Youth Studio Classes in fall, winter, and spring for ages 6–15, or take a Summer Art Camp class. Scholarships are available.

Museum of Wisconsin Art ($$) 🏠 🔥

205 Veterans Ave.,
West Bend, WI 53095
(262) 334-9638
wisconsinart.org
MOWA is the only museum in the world that is dedicated to collecting and maintaining works

from Wisconsin. They offer themed Studio Saturdays every single week for kids and families to enjoy. Plus, entrance fees are actually low cost memberships that allow unlimited access to the museum for a full year.

Don't miss it! MOWA puts on an annual Art and Chalk Fest with live street chalking, face painting, art projects and more.

Art Studios

A Touch of Glaze ($$) 🏠
8215 Meadowbrook Rd., Waukesha, WI 53188
(262) 524-0231
atouchofglaze.com
Choose from hundreds of unfinished pottery pieces to paint, and get inspiration from idea books, stamps & stencils. No reservations or experience required.

Cloud 9 Workshop ($$$) 🏠🔥🪵
5205 W. North Ave., Milwaukee, WI 53208
(414) 395-6922
cloud9workshop.org
Cloud 9 Workshop is a local eco-art studio that offers uniquely designed workshops and parties for children and adults. At Cloud 9 Workshop participants are inspired and empowered to build, sew, print, craft, paint, dream & create. Their most popular workshops include ArTogether for Tots (Ages 2.5-5 yrs.), Art Club (5-10 yrs.) and DIY Workshops for adults. Workshops for children are taught by certified art educators and designed to be developmentally appropriate for the age of the child. All are welcome at Cloud 9 Workshop, and no previous art or craft experience needed.

Glaze Pottery ($$$) 🏠🪵
149 Green Bay Rd., Thiensville, WI 53092
(262) 238-5456
glazepottery.com
Glaze is a walk in paint your own pottery and glass fusing studio located in historic Thiensville. Artists of all ages can work with pottery, glass fusing, raw clay, wine glass painting, silver clay, and acrylic painting. Glaze is also home to The Purple Frog, a parlor serving ice cream, popcorn, gourmet toast, and beverages.

Just Kiln' Time ($$$) 🏠 🔥

N88W16683 Appleton Ave.,
Menomonee Falls, WI 53051
(262) 255-5456
justkilntimepottery.com
Just Kiln' Time offers paint-
your-own pottery, glass fusing,
mosaics, metal art, canvas
painting, and more. Their
business was inspired by their
daughter with cerebral palsy, and
the powerful role that art can
play in the lives of children with
special needs (and everyone else,
too!). No appointment necessary.

La Terraza ($$) 🏠

11520 W. Bluemound Rd.,
Wauwatosa, WI 53226
(414) 443-1800
potteryfun.com
Walk-ins are welcome anytime
at this paint-your-own pottery
studio, and all ages and
experience levels will enjoy a
large selection of pieces and
colors. You can choose from
glaze or acrylic paint on ceramic
pieces like cookie jars, animals,
and candle holders.

Murray Hill Pottery Works ($$$) 🏠

2458 N. Murray Ave.,
Milwaukee, WI 53211
(414) 332-8828
murrayhillpottery.com

The Potter's Shop ($$$) 🏠 🔥

1314 S. West Ave.,
Waukesha, WI 53186
(262) 547-1920
potteryinwaukesha.com
Summer workshops at The
Potter's Shop are taught by
professional teachers in a state
of the art teaching facility where
children can learn the basics of
pottery making and build on their
skills. No experience is needed
and children of all ages and skill
levels are invited to attend.

Young Rembrandts Art Classes ($$$) 🔥

youngrembrandts.com
Young Rembrandts offers weekly
drawing classes that utilize a step
by step method to assure every
student is a creative success.
Children are led to discover that
complex objects can be broken
down into familiar shapes.
They are encouraged to use
problem solving skills and their
imagination to create their own
creative drawings.

Mobile Art Studios

A.W.E. Truck Studio (Artists Working in Education) (*)

awe-inc.org
Seeing the colorfully painted
A.W.E. Truck Studio van in
your neighborhood is the art
equivalent of hearing the ice
cream truck. The A.W.E. truck
studio provides free, drop-in
art activities to Milwaukee's

youth, primarily in under-served neighborhoods. The Summer Truck Studio Program partners with Milwaukee County Parks and Milwaukee Recreation to offer three hours of free arts enrichment activities daily over a six week period in parks and playgrounds throughout Milwaukee, as well as occasional evening visits to various community gatherings. Kids create imaginative take home projects including sculpture, painting, and mixed-media collage. During the school year, the Truck Studio visits every Milwaukee Public Library location. For a fee, A.W.E. will send out a Truck Studio van and team of artists to work with youth at festivals, block parties, fundraisers, and more.

Kohl's Color Wheels (*)
mam.org

A mobile art experience designed for the entire family, the Kohl's Color Wheels van makes appearances at festivals and community events throughout the year, including Summerfest. Kids can participate in free, hands-on art projects inspired by the Museum's Collection and special exhibitions. Visit the art museum's website to find their most updated schedule.

Live Theater for Kids

Brookfield Center for the Arts
2945 N. Brookfield Rd., Brookfield, WI 53045
(262) 923-7107
brookfieldcenterforthearts. com

The Brookfield Center for the Arts offers theater classes and productions for kids, as well as music and dance lessons.

Comedy Sportz ($) 🏠 🔥
420 S. 1st St., Milwaukee, WI 53202
(414) 272-8888
cszmke.com

Did you know that the hilarious folks at Comedy Sportz offer a kid-friendly improv matinee each and every Saturday afternoon? It's perfect for birthday parties or scout groups. Plus, during the summer, kids can participate in their improv camp where they learn valuable life skills through improvisation games and activities.

First Stage ($$$) 🏠 🔥
325 W. Walnut St.,
Milwaukee, WI 53212
(414) 267-2929
firststage.org

First Stage is Milwaukee's premier youth theater organization, and it has something for all ages. Its skilled actors and crew put on high-quality shows for the whole family to enjoy.

Luckily, you can start when your children are very young. The First Steps series at the Milwaukee Youth Arts Center presents short and interactive plays suited for children ages 3 to 6. The atmosphere is casual and friendly, so you don't have to worry if your child speaks a little too loudly or has to use the restroom during the performance. There's even a talk back feature where kids can ask questions of the cast. As your child gets to school age, the shows in The Family Series at the Todd Wehr Theater will be just right.

If your child has a special need, check their schedule for regular sensory friendly performances that feature a smaller audience size, fewer loud sounds and bright lights, designated quiet areas, and more.

In addition to their performances, after school and summer theater classes are offered starting at age three for all abilities. The First Stage Young Company is an advanced actor training program for high school students that presents a full-scale productions each season.

Did you know? First Stage offers "Pay What You Choose" performances throughout the year, for which they suggest a minimum five dollar donation.

Schauer Arts & Activities Center ($$)
147 N. Rural St.,
Hartford, WI 53027
(262) 670-0560
schauercenter.org
This performing arts center about 40 minutes northwest of Milwaukee presents family-friendly performances throughout the year.

Skylight Music Theater ($$$)

Broadway Theatre Center
158 N. Broadway,
Milwaukee, WI 53202
(414) 291-7811
skylightmusictheatre.org

Skylight Music Theatre owns and operates the Broadway Theatre Center which houses the 358-seat European style Cabot Theatre and a 99-seat black box Studio Theatre. They specialize in music theatre ranging from opera to Broadway musicals. Check their updated schedule online to find current family-friendly shows.

Sunset Playhouse ($) 🎂 🔥

800 Elm Grove Rd.,
Elm Grove, WI 53122
(262) 782-4431
sunsetplayhouse.com

Sunset Playhouse puts on live shows for kids such as "Into the Woods, Jr." and "Aesop's Tales: Aesop's Fables." They also offer an opportunity for kids ages 7th grade to 12th grade to put on a junior musical. You'll find theater classes and camps for kids as young as two years old, such as improvisation, stage combat, and musical theater.

One of their best programs for young children is their Bug in a Rug Children's Theatre. The shows offer an interactive experience for the whole family to enjoy (in their pajamas!), and it's geared specifically towards kids ages 3-8. The shows are funny and age-appropriate, and the audience gets to participate often. Bring your blankets, pillows, and stuffed animals, and get ready to snuggle.

Wilson Center for the Arts ($$) 🎂 🔥

19805 W. Capitol Dr.,
Brookfield, WI 53045
(262) 781-9470
wilson-center.com

The Wilson Center offers a variety of performances and events that the whole family can enjoy throughout the year. The Tales by the Fire Series includes three one-hour performances that are fun and age-appropriate, and it takes place in their modern but cozy grand atrium.

Kid-friendly Museums

Long gone are the days of quiet, stuffy museums. The Milwaukee area boasts a wide variety of kid-friendly museums that are exciting, modern, and hands-on.

Quick reference - Free admission days

Betty Brinn Children's Museum: Free admission for all on the third Thursday of every month from 5:00 p.m. - 8:00 p.m.

The Domes: Free on first Thursdays with proof of county residency (excluding major holidays).

Harley-Davidson Museum: Children under 5 always free.

Milwaukee Art Museum: Children 12 and under always free. Free admission first Thursday of each month.

Milwaukee Public Museum: Free general admission on the first Thursday of each month.

Art Museums

Read about Lynden Sculpture garden, the Milwaukee Art Museum, and the Museum of Wisconsin Art in "Exploring the arts with kids." (Pg. 93)

Natural History and Science Museums

Dinosaur Discovery Museum (*) 🏛️ 🔥
5608 Tenth Ave., Kenosha, WI 53140
(262) 653-4450
kenosha.org/wp-dinosaur
Just a few blocks from Lake Michigan in downtown Kenosha, and about a 45 minute drive from downtown Milwaukee, you'll find the free Dinosaur

102

Discovery Museum. The museum is small, but it's worth a stop on a day trip to Kenosha or if you happen to be in the area.

The main gallery is filled with casts of actual dinosaur fossil bones, and each one is labeled with information. Kids learn how we know they existed, what they looked like, how they behaved, and what happened to them. You can also listen to environmental and animal sounds of the Mesozoic era.

Helpful Hint: Don't leave without heading downstairs where you'll find dinosaur themed crafts, floor puzzles, and activities. You'll even find a place where young children can dig for pretend fossils. Catch a peek into an on-site laboratory which runs in association with the Carthage Institute of Paleontology.

Milwaukee Public Museum ($$$) 🏠 🔥

800 W. Wells St.,
Milwaukee, WI 53233
(414) 278-2728
mpm.edu

One of the most beloved exhibits is the immersive Streets of Old Milwaukee, originally opened

in 1965, and renovated for its 50th anniversary in 2015. After entering through an old-fashioned street car, visitors get a glimpse of what life was like in Milwaukee in the 1800's by strolling along cobblestone streets and peering through dozens of store-front windows and residences. The grandmother resting in her rocking chair is a local celebrity. (She even has her own Twitter account!) You can make the most of your visit by downloading the Streets of Old Milwaukee app, which allows you to pick a Streets resident to be your tour guide.

Other must-visit exhibits include the European Village, which brings 33 immigrant cultures to life at the turn of the 19th century and the Butterfly Vivarium, where butterflies flutter freely and kids can try on costumes and participate in hands-on activities. *Pro tip:* wear red or orange to attract the butterflies!

Did you know?
-Visitors can see the skeleton of the Hebior Mammoth without even paying admission. The exhibit is open to the public on the ground floor. The mammoth is over 14,000 years old and was found in Kenosha County. It's notable especially because it helps date human habitation in our region of North America.

-The museum has 234 solar panels on its south-facing tower wall. You can learn more about the green roof in the exhibit Meadows in the Sky: The Green Roof, also free and accessible to the public at any time.

-The Milwaukee Public Museum planetarium is the first in the world to debut a Digistar 6 computer projection system. The Dome Theater boasts a six-story-tall screen and digital surround sound, and delights families with stunning 3D animations and vistas of the night sky, Mt. Everest, dinosaur life, and more!

-You can explore the exhibits by flashlight at night during a museum overnight. There's a different theme each month!

Fun fact: There are three secret buttons in the Milwaukee Public Museum. The most widely known one is found by the Bison Hunt exhibit. If you press it, you'll activate a rattlesnake noise and movement. Another is found in the Rainforest exhibit near the howler monkey. And the final one is found in the Exploring Life on Earth exhibit.

Get in free! Milwaukee County Residents receive free admission on Thursdays and a $2.00 discount on admission every day.

North Point Lighthouse ($) 🧁
2650 N. Wahl Ave.,
Milwaukee, WI 53211
(414) 332-6754
northpointlighthouse.org
Located between two ravines in Lake Park, the charming North Point Lighthouse Museum was built in 1855. It has been restored to its original old world charm, and today you can visit to learn all about Milwaukee's famous lighthouse and its keepers. Visitors can explore the maritime history of the Great Lakes through artifacts and exhibits, such as the lighthouse keeper's original ledgers from the 1800's and an 800 pound brass fog bell. You can admire the Queen Anne-style Keeper's Quarters, and climb the 74 foot tall tower for a stunning view of Lake Michigan, Milwaukee & Lake Park. (Children must be at least 5 years old and at least 38 inches tall to climb the tower.)

Museum of Quilts and Fiber Arts
N50 W5050 Portland Rd.,
Cedarburg, WI 53012
(262) 546-0300
wiquiltmuseum.com
The museum, located on a picturesque historic farmstead, showcases intricate needlework and textiles of all kinds. Check their website to find out about current exhibits.

Get in free: The Museum of Quilts and Fiber Arts hosts a few Family Free Days throughout the year which feature art projects, scavenger hunts, and other kid-friendly games and activities.

Living History Museums

Top pick: Old World Wisconsin ($$) 🔥

W372 S9727 Wisconsin 67, Eagle, WI 53119
(262) 594-6301
oldworldwisconsin.
wisconsinhistory.org

Old World Wisconsin brings 19th century history to life like no other place in Wisconsin. In fact, it's the largest outdoor museum of rural life in the entire country. Original structures from across the region were painstakingly dismantled and reconstructed to build this 600-acre open-air museum. There are over 60 buildings to explore including a schoolhouse, church, and furnished houses.

In the Crossroad Village, visitors can learn iron-crafting techniques, watch shoemaking

demonstrations, and experience what a typical church experience was like. On the farmsteads, you'll see horses, roosters, pigs, sheep, and other livestock, and learn about old-fashioned farm machinery, tools, and agricultural techniques.

Throughout the experience, visitors will learn about food preparation and preservation techniques in a world of harsh winters. You'll see authentic wood stoves, outdoor cooking demonstrations, and learn about holiday food traditions. You can also learn about gardening techniques and stroll through beautifully maintained heirloom gardens, filled with lavender, herbs and seasonal produce.

The best part about a visit to Old World Wisconsin is participating in hands-on activities including ice cream making, crafts, outdoor games, churning butter, domestic chores, and walking on wooden stilts. They also host vintage baseball games during the summer.

New Berlin Historical Park (*)

19765 W. National Ave., New Berlin, WI 53146
(262) 643-8855
newberlinhistoricalsociety.org

Tour the grounds anytime on the Prospect Hill Settlement District and explore the former Freewill Baptist Church building, a carriage house and barn, a little red schoolhouse, the Alice Weston Memorial Garden, the Weston Antique

Orchard, a gazebo, a charming log cabin, an old-fashioned windmill, two former homes, and a small museum.

Old Falls Village Museum (*)

N96 W15791 County Line Rd., Germantown, WI 53022
(262) 532-4775
oldfallsvillage.com
Nestled on the grounds of a beautiful 17-acre park, Old Falls Village is a 17-acre park that features a log home, school house, barn, railroad depot, antiques, and artifacts from the 19th century. The highlight of the park is the 1858 Miller-Davidson House, which is listed on the National Register of Historic Places.

Pioneer Village ($)

4880 County Road I,
Saukville, WI 53080
(262) 377-4510
co.ozaukee.wi.us
Pioneer Village features 17 buildings from the 19th century, including fully furnished homes, barns, and the original Cedarburg Railroad Depot. Check their website for tour times and special family-friendly events.

Trimborn Farm ($)

8881 W. Grange Ave.,
Greendale, WI 53129
(414) 273-8288
trimbornfarm.com
Trimborn Farm is the only Milwaukee County Park with a historic theme. It includes a Cream City brick farmhouse,

one of the last and largest stone barns in Wisconsin, a worker's bunkhouse, threshing barn, and 75-foot kiln. The park is open every day to take a walk or read a book, but the buildings are open only by appointment.

More Museums

Betty Brinn Children's Museum ($)

929 E. Wisconsin Ave.,
Milwaukee, WI 53202
(414) 390-5437
bbcmkids.org
Betty Brinn Children's Museum offers something hands-on and interactive for all ages. The youngest visitors can visit Pocket Park, where they can climb the tree house puppet theater, dig and plant in the garden bed, fish in a pretend pond, sift and scoop in the sandbox, and more.

School-aged kids will love the Home Town Village, where they can role play in a kid-size, authentic-feeling grocery store, news station with anchor desk, construction site, bank and teller window, city bus, and more. Kids can also learn about health and nutrition through interactive games in the Kohl's Healthy Kids area. The drive-thru window is an especially fun way to practice making healthy choices.

Stop by the Be a Maker space to create a unique do-it-yourself project that you can take home, using their tools, materials and technologies.

In the warmer months, be sure to check out their Bugs on the Balcony exhibit outside. Kids can build a bug or climb a giant bee hive, all while learning more about insects.

Check their website for visiting exhibits.

Get in free: The Betty Brinn Children's Museum offers an evening of free admission on the third Thursday of each month called Neighborhood Night.

Chudnow Museum of Yesteryear ($)

839 North 11th St.,
Milwaukee, WI 53233
(414) 273-1680
chudnowmuseum.org

The Chudnow Museum of Yesteryear brings the 1920's and 30's in Milwaukee to life, thanks to Avrum Chudnow's (1913-2005) eclectic collection of over 250,000 artifacts from those years. Parking is free, and it will take you an hour or so to walk through and explore the exhibits. You'll see an old fashioned grocery store and depot, as well as fascinating items like old-fashioned telephones, candy, scales, pianos, and signs from a bygone era. (One reads: "From the makers of aspirin, introducing...Heroin. For non-addictive relief of the coughs since 1889.") A trip here is the closest you can get to actually traveling back in time.

Milwaukee Fire Museum (*)

1615 W. Oklahoma Ave.,
Milwaukee, WI 53215
(414) 286-5272
city.milwaukee.gov

Built in 1927, this museum houses the first department ambulance, a 1947 Cadillac, plus two trucks built in the Milwaukee Fire Department Shop during the 1920's and 30's. It also features a vintage bunk room, kitchen, locker room, hose tower, dormitory style bunk-room, alarm area, and a fire officer's office. Admission is free, but hours are limited, so check their website first.

Harley-Davidson Museum ($$)

400 W. Canal St.,
Milwaukee, WI 53201
(414) 287-2789
harley-davidson.com/museum

The Harley-Davidson Museum is not just for big, bad biker types. The whole family will love the colorful, interactive exhibits. You'll see vintage police bikes, real motorcycle engines, the Rhinestone Harley, the Elvis bike, a multi-colored tank wall, and the oldest known motorcycle in existence.

Visit the Imagination Station, where kids can dress up in Harley gear and explore games, puzzles, and activities. Look for the discovery drawers and rummage through vintage toys and collectibles from a by-gone era. There's even an interactive station to build your own bike and an Evil Knieval throwback arcade game.

But you can't leave without saddling up in the Experience Gallery, where you'll find dozens of models on which to climb and pretend to ride.

If you're hungry after the museum, grab a bite to eat at Motor Bar & Restaurant, which offers lots of options for kids.

Mitchell Gallery of Flight (*)

5300 S. Howell Ave., Milwaukee, WI 53207
(414) 747-4503
mitchellgallery.org

If you find yourself at the airport with some time to spend, stop by this small non-profit aviation museum. The Mitchell Gallery of Flight houses local aviation models, memorabilia, and photographs.

Tours and Tastings

Local tours and tastings are a great way to break the monotony of typical weekend activities. You'll learn something new, support local companies and products, and have fun doing it. The tours and tastings in this chapter are all kid-friendly, so have fun exploring!

88Nine Studio (*)

220 E. Pittsburgh Ave.,
Milwaukee, WI 53204
(414) 892-8900
radiomilwaukee.org

Check out 88Nine's custom-built studio in Walker's Point every Thursday at 4:30 p.m. (except on major holidays). You'll get a "behind the scenes" 30-minute tour of the sound-proof recording studios, the 100-seat performance space, and the 2,500 square foot Green Roof that can hold up to 1,500 gallons of rainwater. The roof provides a unique view of downtown Milwaukee, including the Hoan Bridge, the Marcus Amphitheater, and Walker's Point. After the tour, you can stay for the free 414 Music Live performance or grab a warm drink at Stone Creek Coffee's Radio Milwaukee Cafe. Reserve a spot for your tour on their website.

Basilica of St. Josaphat (*)

2333 S. 6th St.,
Milwaukee, WI 53215
(414) 645-5623
thebasilica.org

The Basilica of St. Josaphat was completed in 1901, and it serves as a testament to the early Polish immigrants of Milwaukee. The opulent and impressive Basilica is open Monday through Saturday for visits, and you can pick up a walking tour brochure at the Visitor Center. There is also a free exhibit on the lower level of the Pavilion that includes images and information detailing the story of the Basilica.

Central Library (*)

814 W. Wisconsin Ave.,
Milwaukee, WI 53233
(414) 286-TOUR (8687)
mpl.org

Central Library opened its doors in October of 1898 in response to the Milwaukee Public Library's need for more space. It is a combination of French and Italian Renaissance styles and it's built of Bedford limestone. The building has been designated a landmark by the Milwaukee Historic Preservation Commission and is listed on the National Register of Historic Places. The Friends of Milwaukee Public Library offer free tours that start at 11:00 a.m. every Saturday morning in the rotunda. You can also make an appointment for a tour by calling the number listed above.

Cheese Factory Tour at Clock Shadow Creamery ($)

138 W. Bruce St.,
Milwaukee, WI 53204
(414) 273-9711
clockshadowcreamery.com

Looking for an original educational experience? Why not learn about one of the most delicious products that Wisconsin has to offer? Visit this local cheese factory and learn about the history of cheese making, plus answer age-old mysteries like: "Why are cheese curds squeaky?" and "Why is Cheddar cheese yellow?" You'll also get to sample fresh cheese.

Doors Open Milwaukee (*)

Annual event held in September

doorsopenmilwaukee.org

On one weekend in September, Doors Open Milwaukee opens the doors to over 100 wonderful buildings free-of-charge to the public. The buildings include churches, theaters, museums, hotels, universities, and office buildings, and all of them hold hidden treasures and interesting stories. Doors Open Milwaukee designates several sites of special interest to families with children during the event. You can pick up a free passport and have them stamped as you visit each site.

Firehouse Tours (*) 🎂

Contact your local fire department for a kid-friendly tour! You'll get to climb on the fire trucks, try on a fire coat and learn all about fire safety. You might also get a fire hat, a coloring book, and other fun kid swag.

Hispanic Heritage Self-Guided Tour (*)

United Community Center, 1028 S. 9th St., Milwaukee, WI 53204
(414) 384-3100
unitedcc.org

Find the self-guided mural tour on the United Community Center's website. Marvel upon and learn about the colorful murals that pay homage to Hispanic heritage.

Miller Park ($$) 🎂 🔥

1 Brewers Way, Milwaukee, WI 53214
(414) 902-4400
milwaukee.brewers.mlb.com

Get a behind-the-scenes look at this impressive Milwaukee landmark. The Classic Tour includes a visit to the Visitor's Clubhouse, bullpen, the exclusive Club Level, Uecker's Broadcast Booth, and more.

Self-guided Walking Tours (*)

gpsmycity.com

Milwaukee is home to statues, monuments, and architecture that entertains, inspires, and honors our heroes. There are also very unusual statues such as a monument to a duck and its ducklings. Head to gpsmycity.com for seven self-guided walking tours of Milwaukee so you can learn more.

Sprecher Brewing Company ($)

701 W. Glendale Ave., Milwaukee, WI 53209
(414) 964-7837
sprecherbrewery.com

On this family-friendly tour, you'll visit the brew house and discover how Sprecher revives Old World brewing traditions that made Milwaukee famous. You'll get to stroll through the lager cellar and see the Bavarian murals on display on the bottling room wall. After the brewery tour, you can spend some time in Sprecher's indoor beer garden, with music and samples from any of up to

20 beers and 10 gourmet sodas on draught.

St. Joan of Arc Chapel (*)

Marquette University Campus
marquette.edu/chapel
Could this be the oldest building in Milwaukee? Was it actually built in France? Take a free tour and find out the answers to these questions and more.

Stone Creek Coffee Factory (*)

422 N. 5th St.,
Milwaukee, WI 53203
(414) 431-2157
stonecreekcoffee.com/tours
Learn about the history of Stone Creek Coffee, see the farm-to-cup coffee journey up close, and get a behind-the-scenes look at their 1880's factory. You'll learn about roasting, coffee growing seasons, and more in a fun and educational environment. Tours take place every Sunday at noon (excluding major holidays), and you can sign up for them online.

Trolley Loop ($)

milwaukeedowntown.com
During the summer, use the Milwaukee Trolly Loop to connect to downtown Milwaukee's festivals, museums, shops and events. There are 30 stops on the route that link you to major attractions. Rides are only $1 per trip.

Wisconsin Humane Society (*)

4500 W. Wisconsin Ave.,
Milwaukee, WI 53208
(414) 264-6257
wihumane.org
Take a behind the scenes tour of the Wisconsin Humane Society to learn how shelter staff and volunteers help transform unwanted companion animals into much loved family members, and how injured and orphaned wild animals get a second chance. Your guide will take you through the Wildlife Gallery, Veterinary Hospital, Guest Lodging and Adoption Avenue. Weekend tours are free and open to the public.

Green Roof tours of Central Library (*)

814 W. Wisconsin Ave.,
Milwaukee, WI 53233
(414) 286-3030
mpl.org
Get a tour of Central Library's unique green roof. They run late April through October, typically Wednesdays at noon and Saturdays at 10:00 a.m.. Check their website for the most updated schedule.

Kid-friendly Gardens & Urban Farms

Alice's Garden Urban Farm (*) ♨
2136 N. 21st St.,
Milwaukee, WI 53205
(414) 687-0122
alicesgardenmke.com

Alice's Garden is a two-acre urban garden that is committed to wellness and community. You can check their website for upcoming events such as yoga classes and movie nights, or you can drop by with your children and take a walk in the labyrinth. This space is peaceful, relaxing, and really special.

Boerner Botanical Gardens ($)
Whitnall Park
9400 Boerner Dr.,
Hales Corners, WI 53130
(414) 525-5650
boernerbotanicalgardens.org
Explore with your kids to find colorful rose, peony, annual, and perennial gardens, a fragrant herb garden, a daylily path, a serene rock garden with trickling streams and waterfalls, a regal shrub mall, an expansive arboretum, and a bog walk.

The gardens offer kid-friendly programming throughout the year including nature-inspired crafts, and "Enchanted Evenings in the Gardens." They have also hosted China Lights, an impressive Chinese lantern festival.

Get in free: The Gardens typically offer free admission to Milwaukee County residents with proof of residency on the first Tuesday of each month, May through September. Check their website for the most updated information.

112

Buds n' Sprouts Kids Garden (*)

Havenwoods State Forest
6141 N Hopkins St.,
Milwaukee, WI 53209
(414) 527-0232
friendsofhavenwoods.org/nitc-gardens.html

Havenwoods State Forest is home to a huge garden space where kids can discover nature. In the Buds n' Sprouts Kids Garden, they can jump from plant to plant, collect bugs, watch worms, and sniff the colorful flowers. Nearby, the Heritage Gardens feature traditional food crops from five major cultural groups in America - African American, Asian American, European American, Hispanic American, and Native American. In the Naturalist's Backyard, you'll find a model landscape with native plants, nurtured by compost bins. There is also a rain garden that uses run off rainwater from the roof to feed blooming flowers vall summer long.

Lamm Gardens (*)

2708 Sherman Rd.,
Jackson, WI 53037
(262) 677-3010
lammscape.com

Lammscape's beautifully landscaped grounds are open to the public for free events throughout the season. Check out their kid-friendly events on their website. In the past they've hosted train-themed events, pumpkin painting parties, and more.

Lynden Sculpture Gardens ($)

2145 W. Brown Deer Rd.,
Milwaukee, WI 53217
(414) 446-8794
lyndensculpturegarden.org

The must-visit Lynden Sculpture Garden offers a unique experience of art in nature through its collection of more than 50 monumental sculptures across 40 acres of park, lake and woodland. They offer a monthly Tuesday in the Garden program for small children and weekly art drop-in programs for older kids. These programs fill up fast, so you must pre-register.

Lynden's art and nature camps for children aged 20 months to 15 years integrate their collection of monumental outdoor sculpture with the natural ecology of its hidden landscapes and unique habitats, led by artists, naturalists, and art educators. Past activities have included hatching and raising chickens, building rafts to float across the pond, creating a civilization on Lynden's back acres, exploring the mechanics of flight or the physics of flotation, digging in the garden or pit-firing beads made from local clay.

Pro tips:
-During your visit, you can check out a Plein Air kit for outdoor watercolor painting.
-Family Kits are available at the front desk and are included with the price of admission. They include a sculpture scavenger hunt, nature activities to complete on the grounds, magnifying glasses, and more.
-The grounds provide a perfect spot for a picnic during warm months.
-Families can snow-shoe during the winter around the sculpture garden.
-Don't miss the whimsical and colorful cow sculpture (actually called Des Vaches: Mo, Ni, Que by Swiss artist Samuel Buri.)

Mitchell Park Horticultural Conservatory - "The Domes" ($)
524 S. Layton Blvd.,
Milwaukee, WI 53215
(414) 257-5611
milwaukeedomes.org
Escape the cold during the winter and explore a sandy desert oasis, a vibrant tropical jungle, and elaborate floral gardens, all in one afternoon! This conservatory is warm all year round, and it's the perfect place to explore plant life in different climates. Find story times during the week, check out the Farmer's Market in the winter months, and enjoy live music in the Music Under Glass concert series.

Get in free!
The Domes are free to county residents every Monday morning from 9:00 a.m. -12:00 p.m.

Fun Facts:
-The domes are one acre under glass.
-Each dome is 140 feet across by 85 feet high, which is seven stories.
-It is the world's only glass house of its shape, which allows a better angle for solar heating and more growing room for tall trees.
-No pesticides are used on the plant material.
-The plants are watered by hand every day.

Nature Centers

Havenwoods State Forest (*)

6141 N. Hopkins St.,
Milwaukee, WI 53209
(414) 527-0232
dnr.wi.gov

Did you know that Havenwoods State Forest is the only state forest in the city of Milwaukee? And that it is Wisconsin's only urban state forest? It offers over 200 acres of grasslands, woods, and wetland. There are four ponds, and one is just a short hike from the Environmental Center. There is also a 120-foot bridge to enjoy, and several geocaches to hunt for.

Pro tips:
-Drop in on free nature activities every month on select Saturdays in the Environmental Center
-Take a guided family nature hike on select Saturdays

-Enjoy preschool nature story times during the week
-Say hello to the small animals that live in the Environmental Center.
-Stop by the front desk to borrow outdoor exploration tools for your hike.

Hawthorn Glen Outdoor Education Center (*)

1130 N. 60th St.,
Milwaukee, WI 53208
(414) 647-6050
milwaukeerecreation.net/
hawthorn-glen
Hawthorn Glen spans 23 acres and offers a Little Nature Museum with animals, kid-friendly paths, a playground, and more. It is a popular spot for school field trips, but the self-guided nature trail and nature center are open to the public in the evenings or on weekends.

Lion's Den Gorge Nature Preserve (*)

511 High Bluff Dr.,
Grafton, WI 53204
(262) 284-8257
co.ozaukee.wi.us
Lion's Den Gorge Nature Preserve is a 73-acre park that occupies one of the last areas of undeveloped bluff along the shores of Lake Michigan. You can explore over a half a mile of 100 foot bluffs that offer extraordinary views of the lake. Take bridges over the gorge or take the stairway down the gorge to walk along the shore.

Mequon Nature Preserve (*)

8200 W. County Line Rd., Mequon, WI 53097
(262) 242-8055
mequonnaturepreserve.org
Stroll through the Mequon Nature Preserve and enjoy a square mile of natural wetlands, prairie, and emerging forest. Check their schedule for special events for kids including an engaging weekly storytime.

Retzer Nature Center (*) 🏠 🔥

S14 W28167 Madison St., Waukesha, WI 53188
(262) 896-8007
waukeshacounty.gov
Explore a small nature center with fish, small animals, and educational materials, plus many beginner level nature trails perfect for hiking with kids.

Riveredge Nature Center ($) 🏠 🔥

4458 County Hwy Y, Saukville, WI 53080
(262) 375-2715
riveredgenaturecenter.org
Riveredge Nature Center boasts a natural, restored 379-acre sanctuary of prairie, forest, swamps, ponds, ten miles of hiking trails, and over a mile of river frontage along the Milwaukee River.

The center is very kid-friendly, with family programming every single Saturday morning. You can drop in to these programs or sign up with a family membership.

There's also a Children's Natural Play Area and Children's Tree Top Library.

They host special events for families throughout the year such as the Maple Sugarin' Open House, Frog Fest, Nature Easter Egg Hunt, and the Halloween Night Hike. But perhaps their most popular program for young people is the Tree Climbing program for kids ages seven and up.

Schlitz Audubon Nature Center ($) 🏠 🔥

1111 E. Brown Deer Rd., Bayside, WI 53217
(414) 352-2880
schlitzaudubon.org

Schlitz Audubon Nature Center covers 185 acres of woodlands, prairies, ponds, and wetlands along the beautiful Lake Michigan shoreline. They have family programming led by professional naturalists for kids of all ages (including babies!). Stop by their nature center to say hi to the critters or read a nature book. Each Saturday and Sunday afternoon, you can see a bald eagle up close at their Word with a Bird program. They run special events throughout the year, too, such as their Fall Festival and Maple Sugaring Festival.

One must-do hike is the trail to Mystery Lake. It has a new boardwalk and is wheelchair and stroller accessible. Frogs, turtles, and waterlilies abound on this route. When it's not rainy or snowy, you can climb the 60-ft Observation Tower for a spectacular view of the surrounding area including the lake. For another view of the lake, take the paved Lake Hike trail and stop by the Milner Lake Michigan Viewing Deck.

Urban Ecology Center (*) 🏠 🔥
urbanecologycenter.org

The Urban Ecology Center is an innovative environmental education organization with three branches, all adjacent to Milwaukee County Parks.

Riverside Park
1500 E. Park Pl.,
Milwaukee, WI 53211
(414) 964-8505
This branch is open seven days a week, and you can spend a whole afternoon discovering all that the sun-soaked, plant-filled lodge has to offer.

Don't miss the Native Wisconsin Animal Room, where you can greet turtles, snakes, fish, and frogs.

Insider tip: You can help feed the animals every weekend at 1:00 p.m. Check their website for the most updated times and locations.

Inside the main area of the lodge, you'll find games, instruments, and puzzles to explore, including a huge floor puzzle of southeastern Wisconsin. The two blue slides have a secret entrance, and the hidden classroom upstairs is home to a mural that camouflages 80 animals. Can you find them?

Outside, check out the people-powered pond, and explore the Habitat Playgarden. Climb the spider web, slide down the otter slides, and play in the Woodland Dune sandbox.

Just west of the main building is their three story outdoor rock wall. In the warm months, they offer free open climbs when you can stop in after work or school, use their equipment, and receive assistance from trained belayers.

Across from the building, look for the colorful river mural, created by students and inspired by their experience wading and canoeing through the Milwaukee River.

You can find more public art throughout the park, including an archway made out of found pieces of iron and steel near the northwest corner of the building, and three sculpture entitled "Walk Like a River."

Discover the huge stone archway at the entrance of the Milwaukee Rotary Centennial Arboretum. (You can see the archway from the entrance of the UEC building if you look southwest.)

If you've got the energy, take a Walk of 3 Billion years, a walking path marked with rock sculptures as high as seven feel tall that tell the geological past of Wisconsin. Starting at the building, go west until you see the first cairn made of 340-million-year-old stone at the gravel drive that leads to the warehouse. Follow the winding path until you find the ninth and final stone structure that's made from rock over 3 billion years old.

Throughout the year, this branch offers exciting events like candlelight hikes, maple sugaring workshops, eco-art programs, and more.

Insider Tip: Head to the rooftop and climb into their cozy tipi surrounded by plants. You can read books, sing songs, and enjoy the unique environment.

Did you know? This is a "green" building? It's home to a huge solar power station, and the hardwood maple floor is made from reused wood that's over 100 years old. The wrap around porch is made from wood scraps from the construction of the Atlantic City Boardwalk. There's also a green roof garden and rainwater flush toilets. (You can choose between a half tank flush or a full tank flush, depending on what you did in there!)

Washington Park
1859 N. 40th St.,
Milwaukee, WI 53208
(414) 344-5460

The Washington Park branch has thriving gardens throughout the park and a Young Scientists club or kids who want to participate in hands-on nature activities. They also have a Native Wisconsin Animal room with a 560 gallon fish tank. You'll get to see turtles, snakes, frogs, and fish. In the summer, you can canoe on the fresh water lagoon, and in the winter, it turns into an ice skating rink.

118

Menomonee Valley
3700 W. Pierce St.,
Milwaukee, WI 53215
(414) 431-2940

This branch is part of an exciting partnership that aims to revitalize the Menomonee Valley. They offer a young scientists club, nature playgroups, family hikes, nature crafts programs, and more throughout the year. Plus, you can help feed the animals every weekend for free.

Wehr Nature Center (*) 🧁 🔥
9701 W. College Ave.,
Franklin, WI 53132
(414) 425-8550
friendsofwehr.org

Wehr Nature Center is located in Whitnall Park and offers families many kid-friendly trails and hikes. The Lake Loop is a one and half mile easy hike that takes you along the shores of Mallard Lake, and leads you right to a waterfall into the Root River. For very young kids, try the Family Friendly Trail, a simple half mile hike on a wood chip path with lots of benches and photo opportunities.

Young kids will enjoy hands on exploration and nature puzzles in the Nature Center. Behind the building you'll find the Nature Play Space, where kids will love climbing on rocks, digging in the sand, and exploring the log cabin.

The Little Wonders program is for two and three year olds with an adult, and NatureNauts offers nature exploration for four to six year olds with an adult. The programs include activities such as animal and insect exploration, nature crafts, and tapping maple trees.

Wehr Nature Center offers special events for families year round such as Frog Frolics, Owl Prowls, Cider Sunday, and Family Nature Yoga.

State Parks near Milwaukee

If city (or suburban) life begins to overwhelm you and your family or you need to reconnect with nature, consider visiting one of the twelve state parks within just one hour of Milwaukee. You can hike, swim, canoe, or just pack a picnic and enjoy the day. Find out more at dnr.wi.gov.

Aztalan State Park ($)

N6200 Hwy Q,
Lake Mills, WI 53549
(920) 648-8774
aztalanfriends.org

Aztalan State Park is a National Historic Landmark where you can learn about an ancient village that thrived between A.D. 1000 and 1300. They built large, flat-topped mounds and a stockade that have been reconstructed in the park. Wander around and get lost in ancient history.

Big Foot Beach State Park ($)

1452 S. Wells St.,
Lake Geneva, WI 53147
(262) 248-2528

This 271-acre park on the shore of Geneva Lake is within driving distance to downtown Lake Geneva and offers wooded campsites, a sand beach that's rather close to the highway, 6.5 miles of hiking trails, and picnic areas.

Glacial Drumlin State Trail (*)

810 College Ave.,
Waukesha, WI 53188
glacialdrumlin.com

Developed in 1986, the Glacial Drumlin State Trail is a 52 mile long bike trail that follows an abandoned railway between the Fox River Sanctuary in Waukesha and Cottage Grove. It runs through farmlands and several small towns, and easily connects Milwaukee to Madison. You'll see abundant wildlife on the trail, including deer, wild turkeys, fox, and frogs. Adults over 16 need a pass to bike or roller blade, but kids do not need one, nor do walkers.

To reach the trailhead in Waukesha, head to the E. B. Shurts Environmental Learning Center in the Fox River Sanctuary. Take the Fox River Trail west to the Glacial Drumlin State Trail, on the right.

Fun Fact: A drumlin is a low, tear-drop or oval shaped hill that formed under moving glacier ice. You'll see them all around the trail, hence the name.

Harrington Beach State Park ($)

531 County Rd. D,
Belgium, WI 53004
(262) 285-3015

Harrington Beach State Park boasts more than a mile of beautiful, clean beach along Lake Michigan. Take a walking path down to the scenic limestone quarry lake. The park is also dog-friendly. For stargazing, visit the Jim and Gwen Plunkett Observatory that has a 20-inch telescope weighing over 2000 pounds. The roof of the observatory is designed to expose the full night sky. Throughout the summer and early fall, the North Cross Science Foundation holds free astronomy evenings that are open to the public.

Kettle Moraine State Forest Lapham Peak Unit ($)

W 329 N 846,
Delafield, WI 53018
(262) 646-3025

Ten thousand years ago, a glacier covered most of Wisconsin. It formed the Kettle Moraine and Lapham Peak, and the landscape that it left behind is perfect for hiking. You'll find kid-friendly trails all over the Lapham Peak Unit, and you're sure to stumble upon a lovely surprise such as a prairie restoration or a butterfly garden.

Start your trip at the Hausmann Nature Center where you'll find a children's interactive area, great views of the forest, and nature exhibits. From there, it's a relatively easy hike to the 45-foot observation tower that sits atop the highest point in Waukesha County (1,233 feet above sea level). You'll see lake country for miles. Another stroller (and wheelchair) friendly area is the Plantation Path trail. It offers almost two miles of paved trail through a prairie and wooded area.

Kettle Moraine State Forest Northern Unit ($)

N2875 State Road 67,
Campbellsport, WI 53010
(920) 533-8322

To enjoy the beautiful Kettle Moraine Northern Unit with kids, you can first head to the Ice Age Visitor Center, where you can see a great view of the landscape and enjoy activities provided by the naturalists who work there. From there, head to the kid-friendly Moraine Nature Trail. It's less than a mile with easy terrain. You can even print out a self-guided tour of the hike that teaches kids about the trees they will see.

Kettle Moraine State Forest Pike Lake Unit ($)

3544 Kettle Moraine Rd.,
Hartford, WI 53086
(262) 670-3400

The Pike Lake Unit of the Kettle Moraine State Forest offers several short and kid-friendly hikes that will enable you to enjoy the outdoors together. Astronomy Trail is a half mile portion of the blue trail that takes hikers on a walk through the solar system. The Boardwalk Trail is another half mile hike, accessible to wheelchairs and strollers, and with an observation deck along the shore. Be sure to hike to Powder Hill, whose trailhead is about a half mile away from the Nature Trail parking lot.

Fun Fact:

Powder Hill is the second highest point in southeastern Wisconsin, and you can climb the observation tower for a panoramic view.

Kettle Moraine State Forest Southern Unit ($)

W39091 WI-59,
Eagle, WI 53119
(262) 594-6200

The southern unit of the Kettle Moraine State Forest is 30 miles long, stretching from Dousman to Whitewater. With kids, you can hike the Bald Bluff nature trail, just a half mile long. It's one of the highest points in Jefferson County and it used to be a signal hill for Native Americans. The Lone Tree Bluff nature trail is also just a half mile long. You'll be rewarded with a beautiful view of the Kettle Moraine's landscape, and you'll learn all about its history through the markers on the way up. The Rice Lake nature trail is also just a half a mile long, and hugs the edge of a small pond.

Kohler-Andrae State Park ($)

1020 Beach Park Ln.,
Sheboygan, WI 53081
(920) 451-4080

One of the last remaining nature preserves along Lake Michigan, Kohler-Andrae State Park offers hikes along sandy beaches and rolling sand dunes, and through pine trees and wildlife. The Sanderling Nature Center is situated among the sand dunes right on the shore of the lake. There are interactive exhibits, nature films, picture books, and a rooftop observation deck. The Creeping Juniper Nature Trail starts and ends at the nature center and will immerse you among the sand dunes. Other short hikes include the Black River Marsh Boardwalk, just a quarter mile hike through wetland, and the Fishing Pond Trail, another quarter mile hike with a flat surface for strollers and plenty of resting spots. The one-mile Woodland Dunes Nature Trail is also stroller accessible, and it starts and ends at the playground.

Lakeshore State Park (*)

500 N. Harbor Dr.,
Milwaukee, WI 53202
(414) 274-4281
friendslsp.org

Formerly known as Harbor Island, Lakeshore State Park is nestled in the heart of downtown Milwaukee between the Summerfest grounds and Discovery World, right along the shores of Lake Michigan. Its 22 acres make up the only urban state park in all of Wisconsin, and it's the perfect place to explore and learn about the Great Lakes. This peaceful urban oasis provides a 1.7 mile hiking and biking trail, water access for canoes and kayaks, fishing area, boat slips, and a bridge that connect the park to the Summerfest grounds. The Friends of Lakeshore State Park offer guided hikes and educational activities for kids all throughout the year. Great views of the city and Lake Michigan have been preserved by not planting many trees and instead fostering short grass prairies throughout the park.

Richard Bong State Recreation Area ($)

26313 Burlington Rd.,
Kansasville, WI 53139
(262) 878-5600

When you first arrive, stop by the Molinaro Visitor Center to check out the live animals, hands-on exhibits and displays, and a solarium with butterflies, play areas, and beautiful views. There are usually nature programs going on throughout the year. From the visitor center, you can

hike a .7 mile-long nature trail that is stroller friendly. It runs through prairie and grasslands, and there's a boardwalk that overlooks Wolf Lake.

Fun Fact: The Richard Bong State Recreation Area used to be a jet fighter base. It's named after Major Richard I. Bong, a Wisconsinite who was America's leading air ace during World War II. Plans were underway to pour a 12,500 foot runway for the air base, but it was abandoned three days before it was scheduled to happen.
A group of locals decided to protect the natural area, and the rest is history.

Did you know? The Wisconsin Explorer Program (Ages 3-12) makes it easy and fun to explore the outdoors with your kids. Make tracks to the nearest state park, forest, trail, or recreation area and ask for a free Wisconsin Explorer booklet(You can also download it for free). Inside you'll find nature activities, scavenger hunts, games, hikes, and crafts to help you explore Wisconsin's great outdoors together. Kids who complete the requirements will earn collectable state symbol patches. Don't just sit there - get out and start solving mysteries together!
Visit www.dnr.wi.gov to get started.

Fun with Animals

Bear Den Zoo
& Petting Farm ($) 🧁
6831 Big Bend Rd.,
Waterford, WI 53185
(262) 895-6430
beardenzoo.com
This family-owned zoo houses
traditional farm animals like baby
chicks, goats, and cows. They are
also home to more exotic animals
like lemurs, kangaroos, and
llamas. Kids can pet and interact
with almost all of the animals.

Concord General Store
and Zoo (*)
N6485 County Rd. F,
Oconomowoc, WI 53066
(262) 593-5400
concordgeneralstore.com
Concord General Store is a
gas station, but it's so much
more than that. You'll find
organic snacks, local coffee,
and a petting zoo. There is no
admission fee, and you can pet
and feed the ponies, goats, and
pigs. It's the perfect pit stop on
the way to Madison, or as it's
own destination for a fun-filled
morning or afternoon.

Green Meadows
Petting Farm ($$) 🧁
33603 High Dr. (Hwy 20),
East Troy, WI 53120
(262) 534-2891
greenmeadowsfarmwi.com
Green Meadows offers a
hands-on, interactive learning
experience that can last the

whole day. Kids can pet, feed,
and in some cases even hold
the farm animals, including baby
chicks, bunnies, and goats. They
can also milk a cow if they're up
for it! Don't miss the kitten barn,
filled with sweet, soft kittens for
petting and cuddling. There are
also pony, wagon, and hay rides.
And don't worry, hand sanitizer
abounds all over the farm.

Don't miss the playground that
includes a fire truck the kids can
climb, wooden wagons, and a
John Deere tractor with a slide.

*Helpful hint: Check Groupon
before you go to save on admission.*

Milwaukee County Zoo
($$) 🧁 🔥 ⛲
10001 W. Bluemound Rd.,
Milwaukee, WI 53226
(414) 771-3040
milwaukeezoo.org

The Milwaukee County Zoo is
home to over 200 wooded acres
and more than 2,000 animals.
You'll come face to face with

giant elephants, looming giraffes, roaring lions, bears resting in hammocks, swinging monkeys, and more.

Pro tip: Before you go, download the Milwaukee County Zoo app. It gives you an easily accessible map of the grounds, as well as educational information about the animals. You'll also be able to see if there are any special events happening on the day you visit, such as Boo at the Zoo or Egg Day. The app will also give you access to schedules for rides and attractions.

You'll definitely want to stop by the Family Farm area where you'll find an animal feeding area, cow milking area, a huge playground, and the Kohl's Wild Theater headquarters. Kohl's Wild

Theater offers live conservation-themed shows and Birds of Prey shows for young kids, and they happen all throughout the summer for free.

For an extra fee, you can hop on the Safari Train that runs through the grounds, feed the giraffes, ride the carousel, get a guided tour on the Zoomobile, see an Oceans of Fun Seal and Sea Lion Show, or get a bird's eye view of the zoo on the Sky Safari.

Be on the lookout for unique events such as Snooze at the Zoo (a campout at the zoo with snacks and entertainment), and Ride on the Wild Side, a family-friendly bike ride through the Zoo, plus kid-friendly activities and entertainment.

Pro tip: Family free days are offered six times a year, so check their website for dates and times.

Nurse in peace: If you prefer nursing in a quiet space, the

Milwaukee County Zoo offers three Mamava lactation stations. Locations change seasonally, so check their website.

Racine Zoo ($) 🏠 🔥
2131 N. Main St.,
Racine, WI 53402
(262) 636-9189
racinezoo.org
This small, charming zoo is home to a hundred different species of animals, and it's perfect for young children who are having a first-time zoo experience. It's located right along the shores of Lake Michigan, so you can make it a full day trip with a stop at nearby North Beach.

Shalom Wildlife Zoo ($$)
1901 Shalom Dr.,
West Bend, WI 53090
(262) 338-1310
shalomwildlife.com
Shalom Wildlife Zoo features three miles of looping trail through which you can walk or drive a golf cart. You'll observe deer, elk, bison, wolves, and more in an expansive natural environment. In the spring, be on the lookout for new baby animals! There are educational exhibits and markers along the way. Be sure to pick up a bag of feed at the main building so you can offer some snack to the animals. The whole experience takes about two hours, so be sure to pack snacks and drinks to enjoy at the picnic areas. You can also explore the children's play area, and a Native American artifact museum. Check their website for seasonal events and

specials such as scavenger hunts, pumpkin hunting, and Christmas at the Zoo.

Wisconsin Humane Society ($$$) 🏠 🔥
wihumane.org
Milwaukee Campus
4500 W. Wisconsin Ave.,
Milwaukee, WI 53208
(414) 264-6257
Ozaukee Campus
630 W. Dekora St.,
Saukville, WI 53080
(262) 377-7580
The Wisconsin Humane Society offers Kids' Nights Out a few times of year that include pizza, a private shelter tour, an animal themed craft, and more. They also offer free tours on the weekends.

Godsell Farm ($$$) 🏠
S105W15585 Loomis Dr.,
Muskego, WI 53150
(414) 425-2937
godsellfarm.com
This family farm is committed to caring for rescued animals and they offer classes on gardening, backyard chicken keeping, and more. They offer unique birthday party options and special seasonal events throughout the year.

Must-visit Playgrounds

Top pick:
Kayla's Playground
(Inclusive playground) (*)
3667-3723 W. Puetz Rd.,
Franklin, WI 53132
kaylaskrew.org

Kayla's Playground looks like a fairy tale dream from the moment you catch sight of it, and it doesn't disappoint. You'll pass through a colorful entrance sign to get into this fully enclosed playground.

From the central path, you can turn right for a playground designed for ages 5-12, or left for a playground meant for younger children.

In the older children's playground, you'll find wide, fully-accessible ramps, a ground-level merry-go-round that wheelchairs can fit on, a special needs swing, two huge stainless steel slides (facing north to keep them cool), a rope climb, a wiggly balance beam, two-height monkey bars, a climbing wall, and much more.

In the younger children's area, you'll find double swings, fiber glass mini-slides, a kid's city hall, police station, and firehouse, a caterpillar tunnel, and a registered Little Free Library. Everywhere you turn there is something interesting and colorful to look at, including tile mosaics made by local kids.

The play surface is cushioned, and the building materials are splinter-free. You'll also find plenty of shaded seating areas for supervising your kids or nursing. Outside of the play area there are several picnic tables and three large, clean bathrooms equipped with changing tables.

A Playground at Malone
(Inclusive playground) (*)
16400 W. Al Stigler Pkwy.,
New Berlin, WI 53151
playgroundatmalone.org
This playground is accessible to children of all abilities, and its design was a truly collaborative effort. Even the students at New Berlin schools got to submit their designs and ideas. It was built during a Community Build Day by hundreds of volunteers. The design is whimsical and colorful. You'll find an accessible merry-go-round, all-access swings, monkey bars at varying heights, interactive sound stations, and tons of nooks and crannies to explore.

Fort Cushing Playground
(Inclusive playground) (*)
600 N. Cushing Park Rd.,
Delafield, WI 53018
chamber.visitdelafield.org
This playground in Cushing

Memorial Park in Delafield is a completely enclosed fort with sandboxes, swings, slides, towers, ramps, and plenty of secret spaces to discover. Enjoy the surrounding park and nearby stream after you play.

Imagination Station (Inclusive playground) (*)
700 S. Main St., Oconomowoc, WI 53066
oconomowocplayground.org
This universally accessible playground in Oconomowoc is huge, fully enclosed, and packed with interesting, sensory-stimulating features and structures. It has rubberized surfacing, recycled plastic composite ramps, therapeutic swings, musical stations, and more.

Possibility Playground (Inclusive playground) (*)
Upper Lake Park, Port Washington, WI 53074
possibilityplayground.org
Possibility Playground was built with children of all types of physical abilities in mind, and has been used by thousands of children and parents to blend the line between learning, therapy and playtime. It sits in Upper Lake Park in Port Washington with a beautiful view of Lake Michigan.

Fox River Park ($)
W264 S4500 River Rd., Waukesha, WI 53189
waukeshacounty.gov
This beloved 257-acre Waukesha County Park is located along the Fox River in the Town of Waukesha. It's just a short hike from the parking area up to a children's play area, where you'll find play structures inspired by nature and a 30-foot slide built right into the side of the hill. There is a small fee to enter, or you can use your Waukesha County Parks pass.

Swing Park (*)
1737 N. Water St.
(In the Multimedia Garden on the east end of the Marsupial Bridge.)
Swing Park started as a few "guerrila" artists and engineers hanging swings under the bridge at night, without city approval. The project gradually progressed as more and more people visited and fell in love with the space. Now the space has been taken over by the city of Milwaukee. It remains there today, offering swings for all who love to swing - and who doesn't? (Caution: A few readers have advised us that it's best to go during the day since the park has experienced crime in the past.)

The Tot Lot (*)
Wirth Park
2585 Pilgrim Rd., Brookfield, WI 53005
The Tot Lot in Wirth Park offers structures that are tailored especially for little kids, hence the name. It's far enough from the road for parents to feel secure giving their little ones room to roam. In the summer, you can head over to the nearby Wirth Aquatic Center Pool afterwards to cool off.

Hart Park (*)
7201 W. State St.,
Wauwatosa, WI 53213
ihartpark.org
This natural themed playground has log balance beams, climbing ropes, a sandbox, many slides, and natural formations to climb on. There is a park pavilion with a family restroom nearby for bathroom breaks and changing. You can also make an afternoon of it by exploring the surrounding park, near two rivers and bridges, and perusing the charming downtown Wauwatosa area nearby.

Helpful Hint:
Cool off in the splash pad during the summer months.

Milwaukee by Bike

Oak Leaf Trail (*)
Milwaukee County's Paved Multi-Use Trail Network
county.milwaukee.gov
This trail features 118 miles of multiple loops through all the major parkways and parks in the system. Loops are composed of off-road paved trails, park drives, and municipal streets.

For more ideas on where to bike (and hike) with kids, check out the section on State Parks near Milwaukee (pg. 120).

Visit city.milwaukee.gov/milwaukeebybike for maps, lanes, routes, and trails, parking, safety information, and other resources.

Milwaukee Bike & Skate Rental ($$$)
1500 N. Lincoln Memorial Dr.,
Milwaukee, WI 53202
milwbikeskaterental.com
See the city from another perspective by renting surrey bikes (family bikes), tandem bicycles, go-karts & more, right along Milwaukee's lakefront.

milwaukee
WITH KIDS

Exploring Science and Technology

American Science and Surplus ($)

6901 W. Oklahoma Ave.,
Milwaukee, WI 53219
(414) 541-7777
sciplus.com

Stroll the aisles in American Science & Surplus and you're sure to find something wacky and inexpensive! This store offers science kits, educational toys, school supplies, arts and crafts items, hobby tools, scales, lab glass, housewares, electronics and more. They also offer free family fun nights throughout the year with exciting experiments, hands-on activities, microscopes, and telescopes.

Discovery World ($$) 🍰 🔥

500 N. Harbor Dr.,
Milwaukee, WI 53202
(414) 765-9966
discoveryworld.org

Discovery World is the perfect place for young curious minds to explore, and their exploration can start before you even get inside. Don't miss the wind leaves right outside of the main building. These tall aluminum columns are made of thousands of stainless steels disks, and they rotate with the wind. The material reflects light beautifully. You can also play on the musical benches surrounding the columns.

Once inside, visit the Innovation Station and try your hand with the flight simulator, construction truck display, and more. Climb the winding staircase with neon lights to the second floor and check out the "bed of nails," made of tiny spikes to teach kids about pressure. There's also a road race simulator, a holiday exhibit around Christmas time, and the Kohl's Design It! Lab, where families can create make and take projects together that vary in difficulty and complexity. They have staff on hand who can help you with creative tools such as hot glue guns, heat sealers, and vacuum-formers. Towards the back of the building, you'll find a huge replica of the Great Lakes, where kids can cause a rainstorm or fog with the touch of a button. Upstairs is a replica of a 19th century Great Lakes schooner that you can climb on board and explore.

On one side of the life-size ship, you'll find the Simple Machine Shipyard, where kids learn about the building blocks of complex machines. Kids are empowered to lift large boulders, use a pulley system to lift themselves into the air, and more. On the opposite side of the ship, visitors can explore how Milwaukee Water Works purifies its water.

Downstairs, the Reiman Aquarium makes the underworld of Lake Michigan come alive to visitors with hands-on and immersive exhibits. Fish swim above, below, and all around you, and kids can pet sting-rays, crabs and more.

Besides Discovery World's exciting exhibits, they also offer family workshops like "Food of the Future" that give kids access to hands-on, super-fun learning.

Engineering for Kids ($$) 🧁 🔥

(414) 247-1248

engineeringforkids.net

Engineering for Kids brings science, technology, engineering, and math (STEM), to kids ages 4 to 14 in a fun and challenging way through classes, camps, after-school clubs, and parties. Kids participate in activities such as building a miniature roller coaster, designing video games, launching rockets, and building robots.

Milwaukee Astronomical Society ($)

18850 W. Observatory Rd., New Berlin, WI 53146

milwaukeeastro.org

The Milwaukee Astronomical Society owns three acres in New Berlin and features several observatory domes and telescopes, all built by its members. They offer public viewing nights during the warmer months, during which visitors can enjoy a tour of the grounds, a presentation on an astronomy topic, and a chance to use the telescopes.

UWM Manfred Olson Planetarium (*/$) 🧁

1900 E. Kenwood Blvd., Milwaukee, WI 53211

(414) 229-4961

uwm.edu/planetarium

The Manfred Olson Planetarium, located on the UWM campus, boasts an optomechanical projector,

LED cove lights, constellation projectors, and four digital projectors that project the galaxy, the Milky Way, and more on the Planetarium's 30-foot dome.

Families can take advantage of affordable Friday Night Movies, free AstroBreak shows on Wednesdays, and free stargazing on the roof, complete with telescopes and hot cocoa.

Retzer Nature Center Planetarium (*) 🧁

S14 W28167 Madison St., Waukesha, WI 53188
(262) 896-8007
waukeshaschools.com/planet
The 40 ft. dome shaped ceiling in the Charles Horwitz Planetarium recreates the day or night sky by projecting images of the stars, planets, the sun, and the moon. The special star projector can be set to show the sky for any date, time, or latitude. You'll be able to see 2,500 stars fill the sky, along with digital video and sound. The planetarium offers year-round public shows and occasional Sky Watch events. Check their website for the most up-to-date schedule.

Volunteering with Kids

Quality family time that doesn't involve loud television programs with annoying characters? A kinder, more empathetic child? Yes, please! These community service opportunities are family-friendly, and can fit easily into your busy schedule.

Sunbeam Kids ($)

sunbeamkids.org
Sunbeam Kids, Inc. is a Milwaukee-based non-profit organization that provides consistent volunteer opportunities for busy families who are looking for a way to get the whole family involved in community service. Register your family for a suggested donation of $20 per child per year, and choose which monthly projects you'd like to participate in. Past projects include making sandwiches for homeless

residents, cheering on athletes in the Special Olympics, making crafts for hospital patients, and more.

Toddlers and Kids on a Mission (*)

toammke.org

Toddlers and Kids on a Mission offers monthly opportunities to volunteer as a family and meet new people throughout Milwaukee. Past projects include toy and supply drives, outdoor clean up days, serving meals at shelters, and meeting up with reading buddies.

Write a letter to a Wisconsin Veteran (*)

jsmailcall.com

The Journal Sentinel's "Mail Call" delivers letters of thanks to the Stars and Stripes organization, who distributes them to veterans on future Honor Flights. Honor Flights take World War II, Korean War, and terminally ill veterans to Washington D.C. to visit their memorials. Plus, for every letter

they receive, the Milwaukee Journal Sentinel donates ten dollars to the Stars and Stripes Honor Flight. You can mail your letters to the Milwaukee Journal Sentinel, 333 W. State St., Milwaukee, WI 53203.

Children's Hospital of Wisconsin ($)

8915 W. Connell Ct., Milwaukee, WI 53226
(414) 266-2787
chw.org

Brighten the day of a sick child staying in The Children's Hospital of Wisconsin. They are always accepting donations of new, un-used toys for the children who are staying there. You can check their wish list online and drop your donation off at the Welcome Desk.

Interfaith Older Adult Program (*)

600 W. Virginia Ave., Suite 300, Milwaukee, WI 53204
(414) 291-7500
interfaithmilw.org

Partner with Interfaith Older Adult Programs to help older adults with cutting grass, gardening, general yard work, raking leaves, shoveling snow, or grocery shopping.

Guest House of Milwaukee ($)

1216 N. 13th St., Milwaukee, WI 53205
(414) 345-3240
guesthouseofmilwaukee.org

The Guest House of Milwaukee is a homeless shelter and

resource center for men who have fallen on hard times. They hand out around 100 sandwiches per day. Your family can easily help them by assembling meat and cheese sandwiches in a Ziploc bag and dropping them off, but be sure to call first to schedule a drop-off time.

Urban Ecology Center (*)

urbanecologycenter.org
Menomonee Valley
3700 W. Pierce St.,
Milwaukee, WI 53215
(414) 431-2940
Riverside Park
1500 E. Park Pl.,
Milwaukee, WI 53211
(414) 964-8505
Washington Park
1859 N. 40th St.,
Milwaukee, WI 53208
(414) 344-5460

Drop in to one of the Urban Ecology Center locations at a scheduled time to be a Park Ranger. Park Rangers help keep the outdoor spaces clean, safe, and accessible. It's a great way to spend the day outside with your family while contributing positively to your community.

Charity Runs and Races

Ride on the Wild Side ($$$)

zoosociety.org
 The Milwaukee County Zoo is a beautiful place to ride your bike through its winding hills and full-grown trees. At the

Zoological Society of Milwaukee's annual bike ride fundraiser, kids can cruise in the Critter Caravan, a special 2.5-mile kids' route through the Zoo. Their favorite plush-toy animal friend can tag along in a bike basket or backpack. Families can enjoy a post-ride snack, make some crafts and get a temporary tattoo in the Kids Zone.

Briggs & Al's Run & Walk for Children's Hospital of Wisconsin ($$$)

alsrun.com
Support the Children's Hospital of Wisconsin with an 8k run or a 3-5 mile walk. The route ends on the Summerfest grounds with a finish line celebration, complete with kids' games and live music.

On days when Milwaukee weather makes you want to stay indoors, but your kids have energy that needs to be spent, consider one of these indoor playgrounds to lift everyone's spirits. They offer inflatables, play-sets, arcade games, go-karts, laser tag, climbing walls, and more.

Milwaukee

Top pick:
Bounce Milwaukee ($$) 🧁
2801 S. 5th Ct.,
Milwaukee, WI 53207
(414) 312-4357

bouncemilwaukee.com
Bounce Milwaukee is truly a place for the whole family. Not only are adults encouraged to jump in the huge inflatables along with their kids, climb the rock wall, and play laser tag, there is also a full bar upstairs and vintage arcade games to keep you busy. They offer refreshing local products like Purple Door ice cream and a Sprecher gourmet soda fountain.

CMP Tactical Lazer Tag ($$$) 🧁
4905 S. Howell Ave.,
Milwaukee, WI 53207
(414) 483-2222
cmptactical.com

Chuck E. Cheese ($$) 🧁
2701 S. Chase Ave.,
Milwaukee, WI 53207
(414) 483-8655
chuckecheese.com

Lucky Bob's Raceway ($$) 🧁
5822 W Forest Home Ave.,
Milwaukee, WI 53220
(414) 327-4003
lucky-bobs-slot-cars.com
Not sure what slot car racing is? Head to this kid-friendly joint to learn! Race powered miniature vehicles on more than six unique racetracks with your very own controller. They also sell slot cars and parts.

Milwaukee Turners ($$) 🧁

Turner Hall (1034 N 4th St.,
Milwaukee, WI 53203)
(414) 272-1733
milwaukeeturners.org
The name of this historic
athletic club comes from the
German word "turnen" meaning
gymnastics or fitness. Check
out their 26-foot top rope, two
bouldering areas, an 11-foot
treadwall, and more. Check their
website for the most up to date
times that the rock wall is open
to the public. They also offer
gymnastics and yoga classes.

West Suburbs

Adventure Rock ($$$) 🔥🧁

21250 Capitol Dr.,
Pewaukee, WI 53072
(262) 790-6800
adventurerock.com
All year round, you'll find indoor
and outdoor rock-climbing
opportunities for all ages and
abilities. First timers ages five
and up can be a part of the
Clip'N Go program that uses
an auto-belay system. You
won't have to tie knots or learn
commands, and a staff member
will help orient you.

Chuck E. Cheese ($$) 🧁

chuckecheese.com
19125 W. Bluemound Rd.,
Brookfield, WI 53045
(262) 785-1400
2990 South 108th Ave.,
West Allis, WI 53227
(414) 546-3600

Helium Trampoline Park ($$) 🧁

16235 W. Beloit Rd.,
New Berlin, WI 53151
(262) 777-2100
heliumtrampolinepark.com
Helium boasts over 130
interconnected trampolines, laser
tag, an LED-enhanced 30-foot
rock wall, an aerial ropes course,
and huge human hamster balls.
There's even a gladiator beam
where kids (and adults) can joust!

Kids in Motion ($$) 🧁🔥

14135 W. Greenfield Ave.,
New Berlin, WI 53151
(262) 649-3144
kidsinmotionwi.com

Kids in Motion offers a central
space with leather couches for
families to sit or rest a moment
while their kids play. The
themed rooms provide endless
exploration opportunities,
including a dinosaur room,
construction room, castle room,
miniature grocery store, and
more. There is also a soft jungle
gym in the middle for all ages to
run and climb. Every so often
the bubble machine starts up for
additional diversion!

Laser Tag Adventure ($$)
1814 Dolphin Dr.,
Waukesha, WI 53186
(262) 510-2746
lasertagadventure.com

Laser Tag Adventure offers much more than just laser tag. You can mini-bowl, play trampoline dodgeball, play video games in the arcade, or play Lazer Frenzy. When you've worked up an appetite, try one of their hand made brick oven pizzas.

Monkey Joe's ($$)
2040 W. Blue Mound Rd.,
Waukesha, WI
(262) 549-3866
monkeyjoes.com

Pump it Up ($)
195 N. Janacek Rd.,
Brookfield, WI 53045-6100
(262) 780-1010
pumpitupparty.com

Skyzone Indoor Trampoline Park ($$$)
W229 N1420 Westwood Dr.,
Waukesha, WI 53186
(262) 696-1600
skyzone.com

This trampoline park features wall to wall trampolines, a foam zone, a dodgeball court, basketball hoops, jousting beams and equipment, a warrior course, and a free climb course.

Stonefire Pizza Company ($$)
5320 S. Moorland Rd.,
New Berlin, WI 53151
(262) 970-8800
stonefirepizzaco.com

Enjoy a family fun night together at Stonefire Pizza Co. After dinner at the pizza buffet, you can explore 40,000 square feet of games and attractions including a rock wall, bounce houses, touchscreen arcade games, bumper cars, classic pinball, skee-ball, amusement rides, a ninja course, and more.

The Big Backyard ($)
2857 S. 160th St.,
New Berlin, WI 53151
(262) 797-9117
thebigbackyardwi.com

The Big Backyard is especially designed for kids eight and under with huge play equipment, riding toys, balls, playhouses, infant toys, and more.

Veloce Indoor Speedway Milwaukee ($$$)
W229N1400 Westwood Dr.,
Waukesha, WI 53186
(262) 232-6700
velocespeedway.com

Veloce (Italian for "fast") offers state of the art go-karts, both junior karts (48 inches or taller) that go up to 25 miles per hour and adult karts (56 inches or taller). This place caters to older children, teenagers, and adults.

North Suburbs

Top pick: Just 4 Fun ($) 🧁
2100 Washington St.,
Grafton, WI 53024
(262) 375-4507
just4funplayland.com

Just 4 Fun is a large indoor playground with a huge wooden play structure, bikes and tricycles, a small basketball court, a soft play area for babies and toddlers, a cafe and more. It's large enough for young kids to stay entertained for a couple of hours, and small enough for parents to be able to keep an eye on their children easily.

Top pick: Rockin' Jump Brown Deer ($$) 🧁
9009 N. Deerbrook Trail,
Brown Deer, WI 53223
(414) 522-1945
browndeer.rockinjump.com
Rockin' Jump is the newest trampoline park in the area, and it feels that way with its bright colors, clean equipment, and exciting features like an X-beam, Dodgeball Arena, climbing wall, and Slam Dunk Zone. Older kids will love it, and they have special tot times for little kids during the week. There's also a large designated area towards the back for younger kids that's always available with a foam pit, basketball hoops, and trampolines.

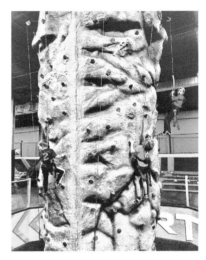

Jumping Country ($$) 🧁
1235 Dakota Dr.,
Grafton, WI 53024
(262) 377-6700
jumpingcountry.com

Ozaukee Sports Center ($$) 🧁
955 Maritime Dr.,
Port Washington, WI 53074
(262) 284-1800
ozaukeesportscenter.com
Ozaukee Sports Center offers mini-golf, laser tag, inflatables, a playing field, an arcade, batting cages, and a pitching tunnel.

Playshore (*)

Bayshore Town Center
Food Court
5800 N. Bayshore Dr.,
Glendale, WI 53217
(414) 963-8780
bayshoretowncenter.com

World of Wow (*)

Jewish Community Center
6255 N. Santa Monica Blvd.,
Whitefish Bay, WI 53217
(414) 964-4444

The western part of the Jewish Community Center is open to the public and is located across from a kosher cafe that is open in the afternoon and evening. Enter through the west entrance doors and be sure to sign in.

South Suburbs

Top pick: LightSpeed Go Karts & Laser Tag ($$)

4251 S. 27th St.,
Greenfield, WI 53221
(414) 817-8888
lightspeedrocks.com

LightSpeed is a true family place that keeps safety in mind for all ages. Hop on their eco-friendly go karts and race up to 25 miles per hour on a one tenth mile horse-shoe shaped track. Each race lasts about five minutes and you'll get a chance to do at least 12 laps. Everyone wears a seat harness, and you must be over 54 inches tall to drive the Performance Karts. For younger kids, there are junior karts that only go up to ten miles per hour, designed for drivers between 40 and 54 inches.

Their laser tag area features a mezzanine balcony, a hand painted space theme painted by a local artist, and obstacles like shipping crates and nuclear waste barrels. The neon patterns on the wall add to the challenge.

In the arcade, you can play Dance Dance Revolution, pod racers, air hockey, Skee ball, and more.

Helpful hint: A day with this much fun can get pricey, so check their website and social media sites to take advantage of deals and special packages.

Fun Timez ($)

6544 S. Lovers Lane Rd.,
(S 108th St.),
Franklin, WI 53132
(414) 235-8675
funtimezparty.com

You'll be busy all day long at this family fun center featuring laser tag for ages five and up, a virtual playground, an adventure jump with harnesses and bungees, and a rock climbing wall.

**Southridge Mall
Kids' Play Area (*)**
5300 S. 76th St.,
Greendale, WI 53129
simon.com/mall/
southridge-mall

Want more indoor fun?
Check out the gymnastics
centers on pg. 180 for open
gym times.

Play Cafes

Play cafes give kids a chance to engage in imaginative
play with other children while parents make friendships
and connections, too.

**Little Sprouts Play Cafe
($) 🧁 🔥**
Shorewood, WI
littlesproutsplaycafe.com
Nestled on the edge of
Shorewood in a cozy and bright
space, Little Sprouts is ideal for
kids 0-6 years old. They'll love the
imaginative toys and inspiring play
areas. Kids can read a story
in the tipi, climb on the wooden

play structure, push and fill the kid-size grocery cart, write on the wall-sized chalk board, or dress up in a fun costume. Check out their music, yoga, and language classes offered throughout the year. In the summer, they offer a day camp for young kids.

Parents will appreciate the clean space, complimentary local coffee, and wireless internet.

Helpful hints:
Don't forget your socks! There are no shoes allowed, but socks are required.

Carry-in food is not allowed, but there are plenty of nutritious and gluten-free options for sale. Ask about the MommyFit weekly exercise class that begins and ends at Little Sprouts during the warmer months.

Roller Skating

Incredi-Roll Skate & Family Fun Center ($) 🧁
West Allis, WI
incrediroll-sk8.com
This family fun center offers roller skating, laser tag, bouncy houses, and an arcade. Check out their website for promotions like family night and dollar night.

Skateland ($) 🧁
Locations in Waukesha, Cedarburg, and Butler
skate-land.com
The Skateland locations are just as you remember them if you grew up in the area. Slip into those orange-wheeled roller skates and bask in the neon lights and pop music.

There are affordable snacks and arcade games, too.

Skate Parks

Cream City Skatepark (indoor) ($$) 🧁 🔥
Butler, WI
creamcityskatepark.com
This recently renovated indoor skatepark features a wooden bowl, street course, and a mini half pipe. They offer special times for kids under 12 to skate with instructors, and they also offer lessons, demonstrations, and other events.

Estabrook Skatepark (outdoor) (*)
Estabrook Park
Check out this DIY Skatepark, located nearby the beer garden in Estabrook Park.

Milwaukee Four Seasons Skatepark (indoor) ($$) 🧁 🔥
Milwaukee, WI
4seasonssk8park.wordpress.com
Four Seasons provides a safe indoor skate and BMX park for kids of all skating levels to practice stunts and tricks. Their ramps range from small for beginners to advanced for more experienced riders.

Tosa Skatepark (outdoor) (*)
Wauwatosa, WI
tosaskate.org
This outdoor skatepark in Wauwatosa was built in memory of a young boy who passed away who was passionate about giving skaters "a place to play." His family worked together with the City of Wauwatosa and Tosa Skateboarders United to build the park. It's located in Hart Park, just south of State Street between 70th and 72nd Street. Skaters will find convenient parking and restrooms nearby. The skate park is open dawn to dusk.

milwaukee
WITH KIDS

Indoor Water Parks

When Wisconsin freezes over in the winter, many of us long for the freedom and comfort of warmer days. Luckily you can always be in 80+ degrees when you head to one of these indoor water parks, open all year round.

Blue Harbor Resort ($$$) 🏠
Sheboygan, WI
blueharborresort.com
An hour north of Milwaukee, it's always a comfortable 84 degrees inside Blue Harbor's 54,000-square-foot entertainment area and waterpark, located inside of a stately resort along the shores of Lake Michigan.

The littles ones can head to the colorful new Toddler Tides play structure for an age-appropriate waterslide and fun spray features. Older kids will love the four-story water center in Breaker Bay with suspension bridges, cargo nets, and four thrilling waterslides. Two of the waterslides are three stories high! The whole family can head to the recreation pool for water basketball and sea creatures you can climb on. There's also a leisure river and whirlpool when you're ready to relax.

If you want to feel like a VIP, rent a private cabana for your family right alongside the water park. Lounge on comfortable furniture, and enjoy a flat screen television and mini-fridge stocked with bottled water.

Head to the Pier Fun Zone Arcade to win prizes, or try your hand at glow-in-the-dark miniature golf. The bright neon balls and decorations make for a memorable experience.

During the summer months, guests have access to Lake Michigan and have a beautiful view of it from the outdoor pool. There's also a lovely walking path along the water.

Don't miss it! *The Riptide is the only double surf simulator in eastern Wisconsin. Use their boards to boogie board and surf on the waves here year round.*

The Springs Water Park ($$$) 🏠
Pewaukee, WI
countryspringshotel.com
Over 45,000 square feet of water park adventures await you just outside of Milwaukee at The Springs Water Park. Your family will love exploring the high-speed raft and body slides,

the relaxing lazy river, activity pool with water basketball & lily pad rope walk, indoor and outdoor whirlpool, and interactive arcade. Don't miss the Triple Dog Dare, a 362 ft. long boat slide for up to three people. For little kids, head to Waukesha Waterworks, a zero depth entry interactive area with a 600 gallon dump bucket, squirting water cannons, small water slides, water geysers, and more.

Timber Ridge ($$$) 🏠

Lake Geneva, WI

timberridgeresort.com

Moose Mountain Falls is less than an hour's drive from Milwaukee, and is home to Timber Ridge Lodge's very own 50,000 square-foot indoor and outdoor waterpark. If you're up for a thrill, slide down the 35-foot-high, 300-foot twisting slides. If you'd rather take it slow, the 500-foot Lazy River might be for you. Little kids will be entertained at the Tiny Timbers area with swings, slides, spouts, and a mushroom waterfall. For fun for the whole family, head to the activity pool with a rope climb and water basketball court.

milwaukee
WITH KIDS

Local libraries offer extensive weekly programming for families including storytimes, play groups, music classes, arts and crafts projects, Lego groups, jugglers, magic shows, holiday events, nature exhibits, and more, completely free to you.

Fun Fact: Little Free Libraries are all over Milwaukee, and there are probably a few near you! The concept is simple - anyone can construct a box for books and install it anywhere they like. The signs say "Take a book. Leave a book," and that's just what you should do! Find a Little Free Library easily on Google Maps, and don't forget to help stock them, too.

Milwaukee Public Library branches
mpl.org

Top picks:
Central Library
814 W. Wisconsin Ave., Milwaukee, WI 53233
Drop in at Central Library every single Saturday at 10:30 a.m. for a fun kids program in the Children's Herzfeld Activity Center. The activities are always changing and are themed for the time of year. The programs include stories, songs, crafts, and more.

The Betty Brinn Children's Room at Central Library gives kids their very own separate area to explore. There's a lighthouse to climb, plenty of cozy reading alcoves, 30 computers, and special children's book collections grouped together.

Fun Fact: The stained glass window in the Central Library Children's Room is called the "Hans Christian Andersen Window". It was designed by Marie Herndl in 1896, one of the only women in her field at the time. It was restored for the grand opening of the children's room in 1998.

Mitchell Street Library

906 W. Historic Mitchell St., Milwaukee, WI 53204

The recently renovated Mitchell Street Branch used to be home to a department store, and it's the largest of Milwaukee Public Library's branches. You'll find a bright and expansive space with a high-tech maker-space, laptops for checkout, a children's collection, and a cozy reading area with a fireplace.

Bay View Library

2566 S. Kinnickinnic Ave., Milwaukee, WI 53207

Artist Peter Flanary created three mosaic maps that depict Bay View throughout history. You'll find them on the linoleum floor of the lobby. One mosaic represents Bay View at the time of settlement in 1832. Another depicts the area around 1900, when a steel mill on the lakefront contributed to rapid growth in the community. The third mural represents life in Bay View today. Don't miss the children's area in the library with toys, stuffed animals, computers, books, and more.

East Library

2320 N. Cramer St., Milwaukee, WI 53211

Visit the East Library and check out unique and functional public art with your kids. Artist Ray Chi designed a leaping, circular sculpture that is at once art and a functional bike rack. He also built a living, growing sculpture of a serpent that winds along the ground and grows into a planted wall. Even the entrance of the library is unique, with outdoor seating that is inspired by the pebbles found on Lake Michigan. The East Library offers family-friendly programming all year round, such as pajama story time and family yoga.

Tippecanoe Library

3912 S. Howell Ave., Milwaukee, WI 53207

The newly renovated Tippecanoe branch is home to a "secret garden" inspired by Frances Hodgson Burnett's 1911 book of the same name. It's a lovely outdoor space for children accessed from the children's area. Kids can read, play, and think in this special space designed just for them.

Suburban Libraries

Top picks:
Whitefish Bay
Public Library
wfblibrary.org
You'll love the whimsical and colorful murals in the Whitefish Bay Public Library.

The Children's Tower has a play kitchen, lego table, and grocery store. There are also board games, magnatiles and other fun activities. Don't miss the brand new Krayon Kiosk with 2 i-Pads loaded with educational games, along with brand new comfortable seating for the little ones.

Wauwatosa Public Library
wauwatosalibrary.org
Enjoy a special night out for your family at the Wauwatosa Public Library. Family Story Times are held on select evenings for kids of all ages and their families. You'll enjoy stories, songs, rhymes, movement, and other activities. There is no need to register, just check the website for dates and times. You can also find unique programs throughout the year at the library such as Rhyme Time, story time yoga, seasonal crafts, and more.

Waukesha Public Library
waukeshapubliclibrary.org
The Children's Area in the Waukesha Public Library is on the second floor, filled with window seats, computer clusters, and an interactive play space called 321 Alphabet Square, designed for young children to develop pre-reading skills. You'll find blocks, a play kitchen, a dress-up area, built-in panels with magnetic letters, and plenty of room to move around. For older kids, the library hosts science and coding activities throughout the year.

Movie Theaters

Top pick:
Avalon Atmospheric Theater and Lounge ($)
2473 S. Kinnickinnic Ave., Milwaukee, WI 53207
avalonmke.com
An "atmospheric" theater is designed to make you feel like you're in another place, and you do step into another world when

you see a film at the Avalon. Originally built in 1929, this historic Bay View theater was finally renovated and reopened in 2014. The original Spanish-style splendor is still on display, enhanced with modern features. The ceiling in the theater uses LED lights to look like moorish Granada, Spain.

You can order and eat dinner while you watch your movie, making the Avalon an easy destination for a family night out. Keep an eye on their website and social media throughout the year for special family-friendly events such as Breakfast with Santa and special screenings of kid-friendly films.

Oriental Theater ($)

2230 N. Farwell Ave.,
Milwaukee, WI 53202
(414) 276-5140
orientaltheatremke.com
Built in 1927, the Oriental Theatre's architectural design is inspired by Indian, Moorish, Islamic, and Byzantine styles which include lush textile, intricate tile floors, Hindu-style pillars, and a porcelain-paneled entrance. The three chandeliers that hang from the ceiling are 8 feet tall, and you'll find a hand-painted mural of the Taj Mahal.

Marcus Theatres ($$)

marcustheatres.com
Check the Marcus Theaters website regularly for family fun series such as throwback Disney classics, Halloween, and Christmas-themed movies. You will often find opportunities for free movie passes for the whole family. There are Marcus Theater locations in Delafield, Waukesha, Menomonee Fall, Mequon, New Berlin, Franklin, Oak Creek, and Milwaukee.

Fun fact: There are hundreds of elephants hidden throughout the interior of the theatre. Can you find them?

milwaukee
WITH KIDS

Day Trips

Milwaukee Area

Top pick: East Troy Electric Railroad ($$) 🛒
2002 Church St.,
East Troy, WI 53120
easttroyrr.org

Ride authentic, historic rail cars on a scenic 10-mile trip through Southeast Wisconsin. Board at either the depot in East Troy or at The Elegant Farmer in Mukwonago. Meander through the depot museum where kids can be a trolley motorman, discover the joy of model layouts and learn about electricity. The gift shop features a unique selection of railroad souvenirs for all ages.

Helpful Hint: For even more fun, try the ice cream at the Lauber's Old Fashioned Ice Cream Parlor next to the depot or enjoy a meal at Ivan's on the Square in East Troy.

Cedarburg Historic District (*)
cedarburg.org
Located just 22 miles north of Milwaukee, historic Cedarburg offers fun for the whole family. Browse through the shops in the Cedar Creek Settlement, check out the General Store Museum and enjoy a walk over the last covered bridge in Wisconsin. It was originally known as "Red Bridge," and it's located in Covered Bridge Park near the junction of Highways 60 and 143 on Covered Bridge Road.

The Cedarburg History Museum allows you to take an immersive step back in time. It features a charming old-fashioned ice cream parlor and the Cedarburg General Store Museum, packed with whimsical antiques from a bygone era.

Keep an eye out for Cedarburg's family-friendly festivals throughout the year including Strawberry Fest and Oktoberfest.

Fun fact: At one time there were over 40 covered bridges in Wisconsin. Bridges used to be covered because oxen feared crossing water on an open bridge.

Holy Hill (*)
1525 Carmel Rd.,
Hubertus, Wisconsin 53033
holyhill.com

More than 500,000 people from all over the world visit the Basilica of the National Shrine of Mary at Holy Hill each year. You can admire the beautiful architecture of the neo-Romanesque church built in 1926, enjoy the peaceful environment and expansive views, and even climb the scenic tower. The scenic tower stretches 192 feet at its base, and has 178 stairs. The views of the Kettle Morraine area are breathtaking, and there's a snack shop at the bottom of the steps.

Port Washington, WI (*)
Make your way to the top of Upper Lake Park, just north of downtown. You'll find Possibility Playground, a huge all-access playground overlooking Lake Michigan. Afterwards, you can admire the boats in the marina, visit the historic art deco lighthouse, and peruse the charming downtown area.

West Bend, WI ($$)
Just minutes from Milwaukee, West Bend is nestled in the rolling hills of the Kettle Moraine. One must-visit place is the Museum of Wisconsin Art (205 Veterans Ave, West Bend, WI 53095) which is dedicated solely to the art and culture of Wisconsin. It houses almost 5,000 works of contemporary and historic art by more than 350 artists, and spans 32,000 square feet in the downtown area along the west bend of the Milwaukee River. Expansive windows follow the curve of the river bank. Every Saturday, the museum hosts Studio Saturday for kids, featuring hands-on art projects with different creative themes.

Don't miss the Shalom Wildlife Zoo (1901 Shalom Dr, West Bend, WI 53090), where you can explore over three miles of nature and gravel road on foot or in a golf cart. Try to spot bison, deer, elk, wild sheep, wolves, cougar, bear, zebra, camel and more. There are learning centers and educational signage posted along the way.

Pro tip: You can buy animal feed at the start of your loop. Save some of it for the animals at the end of your tour. They don't get as much so they are very responsive to it!

West Bend is also known as the Geocaching Capital of the Midwest. You can use a GPS app to search for some of almost 1,600 caches within a 10-mile radius. Each year, West Bend hosts a Geocaching festival that attracts treasure hunters from around the world.

Madison Area

Dane County Farmer's Market ($)
2 E. Main St.,
Madison, WI 53703
dcdm.org

The sights and smells of the Dane County Farmer's Market are nothing short of glorious. It is an absolute must-visit place if you're in Madison during a summer or fall weekend. It's held around the State Capital every Saturday morning from late April through early November. Go early to avoid the crowds.

You'll find stall after stall of fresh produce, artisan cheese, local vendors, and bakery. Don't leave without buying the famous hot cheese bread.

Little Amerricka Amusement Park ($) 🧁
700 E. Main St.,
Marshall, WI 53559
littleamerricka.com
Little Amerricka features twenty-six rides and attractions including the classic 1950's Wooden Roller Coaster The Meteor. The unique park features restored rides from classic amusement parks of a bygone era. There is no general admission. You simply pay for the rides you want to experience.

Highway 18 Outdoor Theater ($)
U.S. 18,
Jefferson, WI 53549
highway18.com
Enjoy an old-fashioned drive-in movie on a 90-ft. screen at this seasonal drive-in theater. Snacks are available for purchase.

Henry Vilas Zoo (*)
702 S. Randall Ave.,
Madison, WI 53715
vilaszoo.org
Henry Vilas Zoo is a 28-acre public zoo in Madison, Wisconsin. Owned by the city of Madison, the zoo charges no admission or parking fees. It receives over 750,000 visitors annually, and it houses an African lion, chimpanzees, a red panda, and more.

Cave of the Mounds National Natural Landmark ($$) 🧁
2975 Cave of the Mounds Rd., Blue Mounds, WI 53517
caveofthemounds.com
Cave of the Mounds offers guided tours of the cave and colorful crystal formations on paved, lighted walkways. Tours depart regularly every day of the year. You can also explore the gemstone mine, fossil dig, and butterfly gardens.

House on the Rock ($$$)
5754 Wisconsin 23,
Spring Green, WI 53588
houseontherock.com
House on the Rock is known best for its gravity defying Infinity Room which stretches out 218 feet over the valley below. You'll also get to see whimsical displays and eclectic collections including the World's Largest Carousel, 182 chandeliers, and a Japanese Garden.

Kenosha Area

Top pick: Jelly Belly Visitor Center (*)
10100 Jelly Belly Ln.,
Pleasant Prairie, WI 53158
jellybelly.com

You do not want to miss one of the daily warehouse tours in the Jelly Belly factory. The entire experience is free, and includes a ride on a mini choo-choo train, chef hats, information about the history of the company, videos about how jelly bellies are made, and impressive jelly belly artwork. The best part? Free candy at the end!

Dinosaur Discovery Museum (*) 🧁 🔥
5608 10th Ave.,
Kenosha, WI 53140
museums.kenosha.org/
dinosaur
Visit the front lawn and main gallery to see sculptures and large casts of actual dinosaur fossil bones, and listen to the environmental and animal sounds in the exhibit gallery. Downstairs, you can dig for

dinosaur fossils, do dinosaur themed crafts, and peek inside a real on-site laboratory. There's a park across the street if you want

to pack a picnic. Find out more about the Dinosaur Discovery Museum in the Museums section of this book. (pg. 102)

America's Action Territory Family Fun Park ($$) 🧁
12345 75th St.,
Kenosha WI 53142
actionterritory.com
This family-fun haven features go-karts, miniature golf, batting cages, paint ball and an arcade.

Kenosha Public Museum (*) 🧁
5500 1st Ave.,
Kenosha, WI 53140
museums.kenosha.org/public
Check out this free natural sciences and arts museum with exhibits featuring mammoths, world cultures, Native Americans, zoology, geology, fossils, and fine and decorative arts. The Field Station section offers hands-on activities especially for kids. Take a closer look at insects, fossils, and shells, and identify the neighborhood birds.

152

Brightonwoods Orchard (*)

1072 288th Ave.,
Burlington, WI 53105
brightonwoodsorchard.com
This family run orchard and
winery features over 200 apple
varieties, seeded and seedless
grapes, and pears. There is no
admission fee. They are not
a pick your own orchard, but
visitors are free to roam through
the orchard and woods trail, and
climb the two-story treehouse.

Where to eat:

Mars Cheese Castle ($)

2800 W. Frontage Rd.,
Kenosha, Wisconsin 53144
(855) 352-6277
marscheese.com
This castle-shaped building
naturally draws highway
travelers from all over and
offers tasty cheeses, bakery,
sausage, and more. It's the
perfect place to visit in
conjunction with other tourist
stops in the Kenosha area.

Sheboygan Area

Top pick: Bookworm Gardens (*)

1415 Campus Dr.,
Sheboygan, WI 53081
bookwormgardens.org
What a treasure this place is.
Bookworm Gardens, a sprawling
green space based entirely
on children's literature, offers
free admission and hours of
whimsical fun to area families.

Located just off the highway in
Sheboygan, it is well worth the 50
minute drive from Milwaukee.

Walking from the free parking
area just ahead of the gardens,
you can explore the Magic
School Bus picnic area. Children
will be delighted by a real school
bus with colorful wings that
they can climb around in. They
can even sit in the driver's seat,
opening and closing its door to
their heart's content.

Further ahead as you pass
through the main entrance gate,
you'll be struck by how well
maintained the gardens are. Each
small area of the garden is based
on a different beloved children's
book. You'll find fanciful statues
and laminated books to snuggle
up and read together at each
station.

The "Hansel and Gretel" Learning
Cottage is the main building that
houses a welcoming sitting area
with wooden rocking chairs, a

cute gift shop that helps support the gardens, and convenient bathrooms. Adjacent to the cottage is a lovely brick patio with wrought iron tables where you can enjoy a snack. It's aptly named "The Secret Garden."

Off to the left of the entrance, your kids can dance around on the steps of the "A Friend to All" amphitheater, and further ahead they can dig for fossils in the dinosaur garden.

As you head to the right of the main building and venture further into the forest, you'll find musical instruments to play and a pioneer village based on "Little House in the Big Woods." In this area, kids can go inside the log cabin where they'll find pioneer era dishes, a broom, and toys to play with.

Nearby, you'll also find three giant Goldilocks chairs and three life-size bears in the trees, a place to build fairy houses, and a Japanese Tea House with a special wind chime.

At the base of the path leading up to the Japanese Tea House,

there's an adorable little tree house based on Winnie the Pooh that little children can go inside of. Next door is a huge Magic Tree House, an impressive structure with beautiful views of the surrounding trees and landscape.

Towards the back of the gardens is the Charlotte's Web Barn and Garden, plus an area based on The Tale of Peter Rabbit.

Before you leave, check out the walking bridge and koi pond, where your kids might spend several minutes observing the bright fish swimming around.

There is no admission fee, your kids will be entertained for hours, and picnicking is encouraged.

Above and Beyond Children's Museum ($) 🧁
902 North 8th St., Sheboygan, WI 53081
abkids.org
Explore almost 10,000 square feet of exhibit space on three floors. You'll find a giant pin screen that contains tens of thousands

of movable pins, a community art wall, a sky crawl, a bee hive exhibit, a kid-sized lighthouse, and much more.

John Michael Kohler Arts Center (*) 🏠
608 New York Ave.,
Sheboygan, WI 53081
jmkac.org
The Kohler Arts Center is an art museum offering free admission, free parking, and plenty for the kids to explore. There is an art space just for kids, an outdoor garden, and ever-changing exhibits.

Don't miss it! One of the highlights of your visit might actually be a trip to the restrooms. Colorful tiles and whimsical designs fill the bathrooms so there's never a dull moment.

Lake Geneva Area

Downtown Lake Geneva (*)
visitlakegeneva.com
Stroll through the historic and charming shops and restaurants, walk along the shore path, and relax on the beautiful shores of Lake Geneva.

Dan Patch Stables ($)
7036 Grand Geneva Way,
Lake Geneva, WI 53147
danpatchstables.com
Dan Patch Stables is located at the entrance of the Grand Geneva, and offers pony rides, a free petting farm, and trail rides. Trail rides are available seven days a week by reservation. Trail guides and gentle horses will allow you to explore nature in a unique way.

Animal Gardens Petting Zoo ($) 🏠
5065 Hwy. 50,
Delavan, Wisconsin, 53115
animalgardens.com
Visit this 40-acre venue which is home to The Dancing Horses Theater and Echo the talking and singing parrot, well-known for his appearances on America's Got Talent. You'll find 16 species of exotic animals and over 60 hay-eating animals. Visit the interactive Baby Animal Barn where you can pet, hold, and feed exotic and farm animal babies. Then, roam or ride the manicured trails. You can also hand-feed the deer in the deer park. Venture to the Indian Village, the interactive petting zoo, and the pond, where you can enjoy a boat ride and paddle with the swans.

Where to eat:

Whispering Orchards & Cafe
W1650 County Rd. MM,
Cleveland, WI 53015
(920) 693-8584
whisperingorchards.com
Visit this small family operated apple orchard and cafe where they serve homemade apple cider and offer a free petting zoo. Cats and peacocks roam the grounds, and you'll find baby goats, sheep and large rabbits in the caged area. In the fall, you'll find tunnels made of hay bales for kids to explore.

Green Bay Area

Bay Beach Amusement Park ($)

1313 Bay Beach Rd.,
Green Bay, WI 5430
greenbaywi.gov/baybeach/
Located along the shores of
Lake Michigan, this municipal
amusement park offers a ferris
wheel, bumper cars and boats, a
giant slide, a roller coaster, and
more. Admission and parking are
free, and rides cost anywhere from
25 cents to two dollars.

Bay Beach Wildlife Sanctuary (*)

1660 E. Shore Dr.,
Green Bay, WI 54302
baybeachwildlife.com
Explore the largest park in Green
Bay which includes over 700
acres of urban wildlife refuge. The
park features live animal exhibits,
educational displays, miles of
hiking/skiing trails and various
wildlife viewing opportunities.
It is home to the second largest
wildlife rehabilitation program
in Wisconsin, caring for more
than 4,500 orphaned and injured
animals annually.

Lambeau Field ($$)

1265 Lombardi Ave.,
Green Bay, WI 54304
packers.com/lambeau-field
Lambeau Field stadium tours allow
fans to experience the Packers'
storied facility first-hand and see
several behind-the-scenes areas.
Various types of stadium tours are
offered on most days, and they
are handicap accessible.

Northern Illinois

Legoland Discovery Center ($$$) 🏠

Streets of Woodfield
601 N. Martingale Rd.,
Schaumburg, IL 60173
legolanddiscoverycenter.com

Located near IKEA, this lego
paradise is about 90 minutes
away from Milwaukee. Plan on
your visit lasting between 2-3
hours. You'll easily find it because
of the larger than life giraffe
welcoming you at the entrance.

Inside, you'll find large Lego
sculptures of animals, famous
people, and cultural masterpieces
like Van Gogh's "The Scream."
The cityscape of Chicago, made
up of over 1.5 million Legos,
takes up an entire large room,
and includes moving Legos and
changing lights.

After you explore the cityscape,
you can walk through a jungle

with a life-size tiger, hippo, and swinging monkeys, all made of Legos. If your child loves Star Wars, they won't be disappointed with the Star Wars section, where they'll come face to face with a life-size Darth Vader, Yoda, and more.

Rides include "Merlin's Apprentice Ride," best for ages 3-5, and "Kingdown Quest," great for all ages, in which you ride a chariot through an imaginary kingdom, shooting lasers at enemies in order to rescue a princess.

Check out Pirate Adventure Island, a large pirate ship play structure, plus an area where kids can build their own Lego boat and test it out in the water. Next to the Pirate Adventure Island is Duplo Village, a play space for babies and toddles with a slide and play table with large Legos. Nearby you'll also find a cafe with a seating area, and two large ramps where you and your children can build Lego cars and test them out.

Before you go, catch a 4D movie at the on-site theater. The movies are about 15 minutes long, and there are a few to choose from.

Don't miss the Master Builder who you can see through a window building amazing Lego creations.

Helpful hint: Save almost half the price on tickets buy checking online for specials.

Six Flags Great America ($$$)

1 Great America Pkwy., Gurnee, IL 60031
(847) 249-1776
sixflags.com

You can visit this huge amusement park with over 100 rides and attractions, about an hour's drive away from Milwaukee. If you have younger kids, check out their special areas for the little ones: Kidzopolis, Camp Cartoon, and Hometown Park.

Related: Check out our list of 12 State Parks within one hour of Milwaukee in the Explore Nature section of this book. (pg. 120)

Professional Sports

Brew City Bruisers ($$)
UW-Milwaukee Panther Arena (400 W. Kilbourn Ave., Milwaukee, WI 53203)
brewcitybruisers.com

For action packed, family-friendly fun, the Brew City Bruisers do not disappoint. The four home teams - the Crazy 8's, Maiden Milwaukee, the Rushin' Rollettes, and the Shevil Knevils - battle it out during their regular home season that runs January through May. The competitive athletes and enthusiastic announcers make each derby bout an exciting experience for all ages.

All of the bouts are general admission, and seating is first come, first served. (Trackside seating is available on the floor, but you must be over 18 - it's dangerous down there!)

Pro Tips:
-Save $3.00 per ticket when you buy them in advance (Adults cost $15 in advance; Kids 6-12 and seniors 55 and up are $12 in advance). You can purchase tickets in advance at ticketmaster.com or at the Milwaukee Theater UW-Milwaukee Panther Arena box office, located at 500 W. Kilbourn Avenue.

-If you plan to purchase tickets at the door, keep an eye on their website and social media pages for specials.

Did you know?
The UW-Milwaukee Panther Arena is home to the Brew City Bruisers roller derby team, Milwaukee Admirals hockey team, Milwaukee Wave indoor soccer team, and the UW-Milwaukee Panthers men's basketball team.

The recently renovated facility boasts a state-of-the-art video scoreboard, free wi-fi, LED event lighting, new concessions stands, and more.

Lakeshore Chinooks ($)
Kapco Park (12800 N. Lake Shore Dr., Mequon, WI 53097)
northwoodsleague.com

A charming baseball experience is waiting for you in Kapco Park, a state-of-the-art synthetic turf ballpark on the campus of Concordia University. The Lakeshore Chinooks are Mequon's amateur baseball team, part of the Northwoods League, a collegiate summer wood bat baseball league. The season runs May through August.

All the seats are good seats in this stadium, and you can even see Lake Michigan from the bleachers.

With contests such as minnow, sack, and cheese wheel races between innings, and a base run after every game, the environment is very kid-friendy. You might even get to high-five and take a picture with Gill, the friendly team mascot, or jump around in a bounce house.

Parking is free and easy, and concessions are affordable, offering typical fast foods.

Pro Tip: Sit behind home plate or along the 3rd base line to avoid the sun in your eyes. Don't forget to pack sweatshirts. In the summer, it can get cooler by the lake.

Milwaukee Admirals ($) 🧁

UW-Milwaukee Panther Arena (400 W. Kilbourn Ave., Milwaukee, WI 53203)
milwaukeeadmirals.com

You can catch a Milwaukee Admirals game during their regular season, October through April, and you'll always feel like you're close to the ice in the Panther Arena.

Ticket prices start at $13 per person, but watch for kids and family days when kids get half off their ticket. You can also find concession specials, ticket discounts, and giveaways on their website and social media.

If your child loves hockey, consider becoming a member of Roscoe's Crew Kids Club. For around $25.00, you'll get ticket vouchers, a Roscoe's Crew item, an ID badge, attendance awards, a party with Roscoe and Admirals players, and the opportunity to be Roscoe's crew member of the game and ride the ship across the ice.

Milwaukee Brewers ($$) 🧁

Miller Park
1 Brewers Way,
Milwaukee, WI 53214
brewers.com

Experience major league baseball close to home in Miller Park, root for a Brewers win, and catch a glimpse of the famous racing sausages.

Miller Park offers a special alcohol-free family section to avoid sitting near the rambunctious people that probably resemble your former self. Your kids will have fun meeting other mini-Brewers fans, and you won't feel as terrible when your toddler throws a nacho at the person in front of them. The view's not bad either!

Head for the Aurora Health Care KidZone on the Terrace Level behind home plate. This interactive play area offers kids under four feet colorful slides, winding tubes and launching pads shaped as giant food items, perfect for climbing and jumping. It opens when the Miller Park gates open and remains open through the 8th inning. Plus, the food stand adjacent to the Aurora Health Care KidZone offers a very affordable Kid's Value Combo that includes a hot dog, soda, chips, a special treat, and comes in a clever, ballpark-themed box.

If your child is a huge Brewers fan, they can become a member of Brewers Kids Crew for around $25. Members get free game tickets, Brewers gear, and special perks and discounts throughout the season. In the past this has included a free Miller Park tour, a free ticket to Brewers on Deck, and a Kids Crew parade on the field.

Be sure to stop by the Selig Experience on any game day. This new state-of-the-art attraction is totally free on game days, located in the Loge Level in the left field corner. You'll enjoy an immersive, multimedia presentation that tells the story of former Brewers Owner Bud Selig and his quest to save and promote Major League Baseball in Milwaukee. (Spoiler alert: At the end, you'll have a very authentic-feeling 3D encounter with Mr. Selig himself.)

For families with older kids who want to splurge, consider the Bernie's Slide Experience before select home games. You'll get a brief behind the scenes tour of Miller Park, a few rides down Bernie's Slide, and great photo opportunities.

On one very special night in the summer, you can experience the Field of Sweet Dreams. Camp out in Miller Park under the stars, play catch on the field, watch a Brewers away game on the scoreboard, meet and greet the Brewers Mascots, get private tours of Miller Park, and more.

Pro Tips:
-Check their website for ticket specials and giveaways, including special days when kids can run the bases after the game.
-Arrive early with your kids. You'll avoid the crowds, you'll get a chance to see the vast, empty stadium during batting practice,
and you'll give your kids a chance to run around before the game.
-Don't forget to get a First Game Certificate or pin at the Fan Assistance Center!
-Nursing moms can breastfeed anywhere where they are authorized to be present, but if you're looking for somewhere private to nurse, you can go to the First Aid area on the Field Level, Guest Relations on the Terrace Level, or a family restroom.

Fun Fact: You can find the landing spot of Hank Aaron's 755th and final home run ball? It's located in the Brewers 1 Parking Lot, and there's a plaque to commemorate it. It happened in Milwaukee on July 20, 1976. Go on a scavenger hunt to find it!

Milwaukee Bucks ($$)
nba.com/bucks

Cheer on our very own pro-basketball team in their brand new, 714,000 square foot arena. Be sure to check the Bucks website and social media for ticket specials and promotions.

Your little basketball fan can be a member of Bango's Kids Club for free and receive a special membership card and certificate, merchandise discounts, access to special events, ticket offers, and a birthday card. Upgrade to the All Star Package for about $25 and get all of the perks listed above, plus ticket vouchers, a membership kit, an activity guide, a surprise birthday gift, and pregame warmup opportunities.

160 **Milwaukee Wave ($$)** 🏚️🔥🏕️
UW-Milwaukee Panther
Arena (400 W Kilbourn Ave,
Milwaukee, WI 53203)
milwaukeewave.com
The Milwaukee Wave is part of
the Major Indoor Soccer League
and they currently hold six
championship titles. Their games
are packed with family-friendly
entertainment and giveaways,
and nearly every home game has
a kid-friendly theme. Tickets start
at $15.00.

Your child can join the Milwaukee
Wave VIP Kids Club. The all-star
membership will get them a free
ticket, a merchandise discount,
and a lunch bag. Upgrade to
a MVP membership for three
free tickets, a pre-game clinic,
autograph session with the
players, and more.

Family-Friendly Restaurants

Milwaukee

AJ Bombers ($)
1247 N. Water St.,
Milwaukee, WI 53202
ajbombers.com
This burger joint actually allows
you to write on the wall with
markers, which is great news
for any family with young kids.
There are all kinds of kitschy
decorations to keep you
entertained. Don't miss the
peanut delivery system that
sends you peanuts through a
rocket tube near the ceiling. Get
a free burger on your birthday!

Classic Slice ($)
2797 S. Kinnickinnic Ave.,
Milwaukee, WI 53207
classicslice.com
Classic Slice is indeed a Bay View
classic. The slices are so huge
they can probably feed more
than one child. There are always
plenty of families in this casual
pizzeria, so you won't get the evil
eye when your toddler throws a
fork across the room.

Maxie's Southern Comfort ($$)

6732 W. Fairview Ave.,
Milwaukee, WI 53213
maxies.com

Stop in for Family Night on Sundays when kids 12 and under eat for $1.00, and enjoy traditional slow-smoked Creole and Cajun barbecue and southern comfort cooking of all kinds.

Milwaukee Public Market ($$)

400 N. Water St.,
Milwaukee, WI 53202
milwaukeepublicmarket.org

You won't have to worry about keeping your kids still and quiet at the bustling Milwaukee Public Market, though you will have to deal with some crowds. The best part? You'll find lots of different food options to please everyone's pallet, and you can eat in the casual dining area upstairs. You'll find a local coffee shop, artisan cheese and sausage, fresh fish, soups and salads, a variety of ethnic food options, and an amazing bakery. Don't miss the vegan restaurant with a real vintage bus.

Original Pancake House ($)

2621 N. Downer Ave.,
Milwaukee, WI 53211
originalpancakehouse.com

Expect fresh orange juice, great coffee, friendly servers, especially delicious pancakes, and omelets larger than your head. There are always plenty of families here and comfortable large booths to accommodate squirmy kids. They offer coloring sheets for children and kids' meals.

Safehouse ($$) 🏠

Location: Top Secret
(Okay, okay, it's 779 N. Front St., Milwaukee, WI 53202)
safe-house.com

The Safehouse, if you can find it and figure out how to pass the agent authorization process,

is a unique experience for the whole family. Your kids will love this restaurant meets spy adventure, where every turns presents interactive elements, spy technology, gadgets, and riddles. You'll learn about 50 years of spy history and see the world's largest puzzle wall.

North Suburbs

Dr. Dawg ($)
6969 N. Port Washington Rd. #100, Glendale, WI 53217
drdawg.net
This comfortable gathering spot is a casual place for burgers & Chicago-style hot dogs.

Highland House ($$)
12741 N. Port Washington Rd., Mequon, WI 53092
highlandhouse.ws
Feast on Carribean-style fare with a care-free island atmosphere and plenty of food options for all ages. There is
even a video game room for antsy kids and adults. It's just one mile north of North Shore Cinema making it the perfect stop before or after a movie with your kids.

Hubbard Park Lodge ($$)
3565 N. Morris Blvd., Milwaukee, WI 53211
hubbardparklodge.com
Located in picturesque Hubbard Park on the Milwaukee River, their Sunday Lumberjack Brunch includes warm, fried donuts, family-style plates of pancakes, eggs, hashbrowns, breakfast sausage and bacon, an omelette bar, and a selection of fresh fruits, cereals and juices. The log cabin feel is cozy and inviting for your whole family.

How to get there: Bike there via the Oak Leaf Trail, or park in the lot at the intersection of North Morris Blvd. and E. Menlo Blvd. Access the park and lodge through a pedestrian tunnel running under the Oak Leaf Trail. Your kids will love this short nature walk, and you'll get to burn off some extra calories on the way home.

Mineshaft ($$) 🧁

22 N. Main St.,
Hartford, WI 53027
mineshaftrestaurant.com
Your kids will love exploring the 5,000 square foot game room, and you'll love the family specials and Just for Kids menu.

South Suburbs

Ferch's Malt Shoppe and Grill ($) 🧁

5636 Broad St.,
Greendale, WI 53129
ferchs.com
Ferch's is an old-fashioned parlor serving hand-mixed ice cream creations on a marble top creamery, along with short-order food, flavored sodas, and more. They have a jukebox on sight, as well as their very own movie theater for parties. In the warmer months, you can check out their beachside location in Grant Park.

Fish Fry in the Parks ($)

Whitnall Park Golf Clubhouse
Grant Park Golf Clubhouse
county.milwaukee.gov
During the warm weather months from Memorial Day through Labor Day, you can have your Friday night fish fry in the beautiful surroundings of the Milwaukee County Parks.

Organ Piper Pizza ($) 🧁

4353 S. 108th St.,
Greenfield, WI 53228
organpiperpizza.com
This Milwaukee landmark, opened in 1976, boasts

delicious thin crust pizza and the country's finest organists to entertain you. There is also an arcade and a small merry-go-round. This place is known for being boisterous and noisy, so your kids will likely fit right in!

Did you know? One of the organ players here is also the organ player at Miller Park.

West Suburbs

Dave and Buster's ($$)
2201 N. Mayfair Rd.,
Wauwatosa, WI 53226
daveandbusters.com
This family-friendly chain restaurant offers sports bar food and arcade games.

Stonefire Pizza Co. ($$)
5320 South Moorland Rd.,
New Berlin, WI 53151
stonefirepizzaco.com
Stonefire Pizza Co. was built for a family fun night. You'll find something for everyone at the buffet, and you can even watch a movie while you eat. Afterwards, explore 40,000 square feet of games and attractions including a rock wall, bounce houses, touchscreen arcade games, bumper cars, classic pinball, skee-ball, amusement rides, a ninja course, and more.

Yo Mama! & The Party Room ($)
1349 N. Wauwatosa Ave.,
Wauwatosa, WI 53213
yomamagoodness.com
bookthepartyroom.com
Yo Mama Frozen Yogurt is attached to a unique venue called The Party Room, located in the charming Village of Wauwatosa. It's the perfect place for a birthday party, and it offers a custom-built photo booth with props and fun backgrounds, a large screen television for slide shows, movies, or gaming, a disco ball and custom sound system, and more.

Multiple Locations

Bel Air Cantina ($)
belaircantina.com
With locations in Milwaukee, Wauwatosa, Oak Creek, and Brookfield, This modern Mexican restaurant has a few locations around the Milwaukee area, and they offer a special "niños" menu for the kids.

Blaze Pizza ($)
blazepizza.com
You'll find location at Bayshore in Glendale and in Brookfield. Blaze pizza is completely customizable, low-calorie as far as pizzas go, and very fast. You'll feel comfortable with your kids in this casual environment.

Lowlands Restaurants ($$)
Lowlands Group restaurants strive to bring the Dutch concept of "gezellig" to their restaurants; which is roughly translated as a cozy atmosphere or the warm feeling you get when spending time with friends.

Their food is made from scratch, often organic, and they use Wisconsin suppliers for many products. There is no high fructose corn syrup in their food, and their beef is grass-fed and grain-finished with no antibiotics. They have plenty of vegetarian and gluten-free options, and every choice on the kids' menu comes with fresh fruit and vegetables.

Cafe Bavaria
7700 Harwood Ave.,
Wauwatosa, WI 53213
(414) 271-7700
cafebavaria.com

Cafe Centraal
2306 S. Kinnickinnic Ave., Bay
View, WI 53207
(414) 755-0378
cafecentraal.com

Cafe Hollander Tosa
7677 W. State St.,
Wauwatosa, WI 53213
(414) 475-6771
cafehollander.com

Cafe Hollander Downer
2608 N. Downer Ave.,
Milwaukee, WI 53211
(414) 963-6366
cafehollander.com

Cafe Hollander Mequon
5900 W. Mequon Rd.,
Mequon, WI 53092
(262) 236-0107
cafehollander.com

Cafe Hollander Brookfield
20150 Union St.,
Brookfield, WI 53045
(262) 785-4490
cafehollander.com

The Chocolate Factory ($)
This local chain offers fresh subs
with warm crusty rolls and fresh,
premium ingredients, plus a
delicious homemade mayonnaise.
Top it off with local Wisconsin ice
cream or choose from a variety
of sundaes. If you love The

Chocolate Factory, be sure to visit
the airy Pewaukee location right
along the beach on Pewaukee
Lake. Other locations are in
Elm Grove, Oconomowoc, Oak
Creek, Shorewood, Waukesha,
Cedarburg, and West Bend.

North Star American Bistro ($$)
northstarbistro.com
Enjoy traditional American
favorites along with more
sophisticated fare at this
upscale but casual eatery in
both Shorewood and Brookfield.
Both locations have a separate
family dining room. At the
Shorewood location, the family
section has toys, a chalkboard
and ample play space. There is
a full children's menu, and kids
eat free on Sundays.

Custard & Ice Cream

Be a part of the great
Milwaukee custard debate
by declaring which custard
is better - Kopp's or Leon's?
Your answer will put you
in one of two very devoted
tribes, but you can't be a
part of both.

Kopp's Frozen Custard ($)
5373 N. Port Washington Rd.,
Glendale, WI 53217
7631 W. Layton Ave.,
Greenfield, WI 53220
18880 W. Bluemound Rd.,
Brookfield, WI 53045
kopps.com
Check their flavor of the day on
their website or social media

166

accounts. And don't pass up Hog Heaven, the yearly flavor during local Harley-Davidson motorcycle events.

Leon's Frozen Custard Drive-in ($)
3131 S. 27th St.,
Milwaukee, WI 53215
leonsfrozencustard.us
Leon's opened for business in 1942, and is still owned by the original family. Their custard is so iconic it has been featured on the Travel Channel.

Or, stay out of the debate altogether and head to:

Purple Door Ice Cream ($)
205 S. 2nd St.,
Milwaukee, WI 53204
purpledooricecream.com
Purple Door Ice Cream is located in Milwaukee's up-and-coming Walker's Point neighborhood, and offers hand-crafted, artisan ice cream that is 14% butterfat. They use milk and cream from Wisconsin dairies whenever possible, as well as high-quality cocoas, liqueurs, coffee beans, and other flavorful ingredients. In their shop, you'll find 20 flavors of ice cream. (The salted caramel can't be beat!)

Fun Fact: Purple Door features compostable spoons and cups, flooring made of 72% recycled content, and service counters made from hundreds of spoons collected from friends and family members throughout the world.

Donuts

Cranky's ($)
6901 W North Ave.,
Wauwatosa, WI 53213
crankyals.com
Is it Cranky's or Cranky Al's? The world may never know. But what we do know is that the donuts and pizza here are a local favorite, and the place is definitely family-friendly.

Holey Moley Cafe ($)
316 N. Milwaukee St.,
Milwaukee, WI 53202
hospitalitydemocracy.com/holey-moley/

Opened in 2014, Holey Moley is Milwaukee's only craft doughnut shop. The doughnuts are made from scratch with whole, quality ingredients and offer a range of styles including cake, yeast raised, filled, fritters, and doughnut holes, as well as a wide variety of gluten-free and vegan options.

Their doughnuts are made fresh daily and are available from 6:30 a.m. to 1:00 p.m., while supplies last. They also feature local brews from Hawthorne Coffee Roasters.

The Drive-Thru ($)
1801 E. North Ave., Milwaukee, WI 53202 thedrive-thru.com
Their mini-donuts are made fresh to order, shaken with powdered sugar, cinnamon sugar or a combination of both.

Happy Dough Lucky ($)
happydoughlucky.com
This mobile mini-donut bar makes balls of dough into perfectly shaped mini-donuts right before your hungry eyes. Check out their festival and farmer's market schedule on their website.

Salons for Kids

A Hair for Kids Salon ($$) 🧁
New Berlin, WI
newberlinhairsalon.com
Sometimes kids can be apprehensive about getting a haircut, but A Hair for Kids Salon turns it into an experience they can look forward to. Located at the back of a shared salon space in an unassuming strip mall, you might pass this place over on the

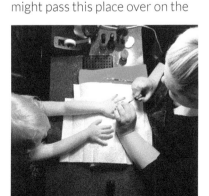

first look. But once inside, you'll see why it's worth a visit. They offer special kids' chairs shaped like Disney characters, staff who work patiently with children, and televisions to distract nervous customers.

If your child loves dressing up and being fancy, they offer princess up-dos that include glitter and special hair pieces, manicures and pedicures in comfortable kid-size seats, and make-your-own lotion and lip gloss stations.

Just Kidding Kids Cuts ($$$) 🧁
Whitefish Bay, WI
justkiddingkidscuts.com

168

Snips & Giggles ($$) 🧁
Oconomowoc, WI
snipsandgiggles.com

Tadpoles ($$)
Delafield, WI
tadpolekids.com

WhimsiKidz ($$)
Wauwatosa, WI
whimsikidz.com

Local Toy Stores

Art Smart's Dart & Juggling Emporium
1695 N. Humboldt Ave.,
Milwaukee, WI 53202
jugglingsupplies.net
You'll obviously find darts, dart supplies, and juggling props at this dart and juggling emporium, but you can also buy kites, boomerangs, yo-yo's, a selection of gag gifts, and more.

Fischberger Variety
2445 N. Holton St.,
Milwaukee, WI 53212
This delightful gift shop has unique finds for all ages, including games and toys, clothing, sewing supplies, and jewelry.

Ruckus and Glee
805 N. 68th St.,
Wauwatosa, WI 53213
ruckusandglee.com
Ruckus and Glee is a quirky and colorful toy store in the heart of Wauwatosa. You are sure to find the perfect gift for a birthday party or for the holidays on any budget. A visit here is hands-on and interactive, and the owners choose high-quality toys that awaken children's imaginations.

The Learning Shop
learningshop.com
With locations in Greendale, Brookfield, and Mequon, This Wisconsin chain is a great place to go for toys that help kids discover, experiment, create, pretend, and explore. Teachers and parents alike will find a huge selection of learning materials, toys, and games for kids of all ages.

Silly Willyz
Pewaukee, WI
sillywillyz.com
This charming toy store is located in the Old Main St. shops in

downtown Pewaukee, right across the street from the beach. They offer educational toys, novelty items, puzzles, games, books, and arts and crafts supplies, plus they offer free gift wrapping.

Winkie's Hallmark and Gifts
Whitefish, Bay, WI
winkieshallmark.com
Winkie's is a landmark in the endearing shopping district of Whitefish Bay, and it has been locally owned for many years. Upstairs you'll find unique home decor, stationery, and other gifts for adults, and downstairs you'll find a great selection of popular and whimsical toys and games for your kids.

Local Children's Boutiques

Goo Goo Gaa Gaa
Brookfield, WI
googoogaagaa.com
This store started out as a baby boutique, and has grown into a lovely store for kids of all ages. They offer fun clothing, toys, and children's decor. They also have meaningful gifts for important milestones in a child's life.

Little Monsters
Milwaukee, WI
instagram.com/
littlemonstersmilwaukee
Little Monsters is an adorable, high-end children's boutique on the east side of Milwaukee, with a great selection of trendy clothing, interesting toys, and even a candy bar. Their Instagram account is fun to follow, too!

Sydney B
& Sydney B Outlet
sydneybboutique.com
Visit this high-end boutique in Mequon for whimsical children's clothes, toys, and gifts, or head to their outlet in Shorewood to save on quality, trendy styles.

Sports & Enrichment

Basketball

Center Court Sports Complex ($)
Waukesha, WI
leagueathletics.com
This sports complex offers basketball leagues, camps, and more.

Milwaukee Bucks Youth Basketball ($$$)
nba.com/bucks
The Milwaukee Bucks offer year round camps and clinics like "Bango's Little Dribblers" that teach the fundamentals of basketball to youth starting at age four.

Running Rebels ($)
Milwaukee, WI
runningrebels.org
Running Rebels is a non-profit organization that offers a comprehensive basketball program that includes academic support, mentoring, and competition.

For more local youth sports and enrichment opportunities, contact one of the recreation departments or community centers listed on pg. 192.

Baseball & Softball / Batting Cages

Top pick:
Prairieville Park ($) 🧁
Waukesha, WI

prairievillepark.com

This seasonal family entertainment center houses five batting cages including slow-pitch softball, fast-pitch softball, and baseball from 35 to 80 miles per hour. There's also an adventure-style 18-hole mini-golf course with water features and a mountain, and bumper cars for kids taller than 44 inches.

BATS Academy Indoor Training Facility ($$$)
Mequon, WI

batsacademywi.com

With over 5,900 square foot of indoor space, BATS Academy offers plenty of opportunity for athletes of all ages who want to improve their fundamental skills. You'll find two 70 foot retractable batting cages, a pitching area, professional field turf, soft-toss batting cage, and state of the art training equipment. Their instructors are available for private, small group, and team instruction.

Brewers Baseball Academy ($$$)
milwaukee.brewers.mlb.com

The first-rate and very popular Milwaukee Brewers Baseball Academy has something for kids at every skill level, and campers are grouped by age and ability. The session includes a trip to Miller Park, where a Brewers coach conducts a behind the scenes tour.

Helman's Driving Range & Mini-Golf ($$) 🧁
Menomonee Falls, WI

helmansdrivingrange.com

Visit this seasonal outdoor sports center to play their 18-hole mini-golf course, practice on the driving range, or perfect your swing in their batting cages.

Hitters Baseball Training Center ($$$) 🔥
Caledonia, WI

hometeamsonline.com

Hitters Baseball is a competitive youth baseball organization competing in major baseball showcase tournaments. Many of their former players go on to play at the college and professional level. Hitters offers year-round baseball instruction and batting cage rentals in their full-service training facility equipped with 16 batting cages, four pitching mounds, and a major league size infield.

Milwaukee Baseball Academy ($$$) 🔥

Milwaukee, WI

milwaukeebaseballacademy.com

Milwaukee Baseball Academy is an indoor training facility for baseball players from ages 4 to 18. Join one of their year round programs for access to a huge facility that includes four batting cages, pitching mounds, a workout area for speed and agility, and a weight room. There is even a parent waiting room with a viewing window to watch your child, relax, and enjoy coffee, wifi, and TV.

River Falls Family Fun Center ($) 🧁

Greenfield, WI

riverfallfamilyfuncenter.com

This family entertainment center has batting cages, plus an arcade and a miniature golf course.

Swing Time ($) 🧁

Germantown, WI

swingtimegolf.com

You'll find slow, medium, and fast pitch batting cages with softballs and baseballs. They also have go-karts for ages four and up, with a minimum height requirement of 36 inches. Their 18-hole miniature golf course has three waterfalls and a 70 foot hole, one of the longest in the country. For extra fun, try the 19th hole for a chance to win one free game.

Bowling

Kids Bowl Free (*)

kidsbowlfree.com

To stay cool and have free fun in the summertime, register your child on kidsbowlfree.com. Registered children get two free games of bowling every single day of the summer. Participating bowling alleys are indicated below. Check the website for the most updated information.

JB's on 41 ($) 🧁

4040 S. 27th St.,
Milwaukee, WI 53221
(414) 281-8200
jb-on-41.com

JB's on 41 is truly more than just a bowling alley. It is an innovative center for affordable, wholesome, family-friendly entertainment. They offer 25 traditional open bowling lanes, a pub-style restaurant, a huge game room with prizes, plus ten luxury VIP lanes in "Suite 41." Families with young kids can utilize automatic bumper bowling.

Don't miss Galactic Bowling when the lights are turned down, the music is turned up, and JB's turns into a family-friendly nightclub.

Koz's Mini Bowl ($)

2078 S. 7th St.,
Milwaukee, WI 53204
(414) 383-0560
kozsminibowl.com

Step back in time with a visit to Koz's Mini Bowl, a truly unique venue with an authentic throw-back vibe. Be forewarned: it's a bar. But the atmosphere is casual, and they have even hosted kids' birthday parties. In the back of the bar, you'll find four half lanes, mini bowling balls and mini pins. The pins are manually set up by workers behind the gates. And you may be pleasantly surprised to find out that your mini-bowling skills are far superior to your regular-bowling skills.

The Thirsty Duck (miniature bowling) ($)

Wauwatosa and Sussex
thethirstyduck.com

You can go mini duck-pin bowling at this funky spot, and the atmosphere is definitely family-friendly. They offer food and drinks, and you can reserve your lane online for added convenience.

Cooking

Top pick:
The Petite Chef ($$$) 🧁
119 N. Main St.,
Dousman, WI 53118
petitechefs.com
The Petite Chef offers cooking classes starting at age four and birthday parties for groups of all ages. In a commercial kitchen, kids learn basic cooking techniques, knife skills, and food safety while being supervised by a personal chef. For parties, you can choose a menu theme including breakfast (pajamarama), pizza, and more. You can also select a general theme like princesses or an Iron Chef competition. All the kids get a chef hat!

Braise Restaurant & Culinary School ($$$)
1101 S. 2nd St.,
Milwaukee, WI 53204
braiselocalfood.com
While Braise does not currently offer classes specifically for kids, children can attend classes with an adult.

Maggiano's Little Chefs
Maggiano's Little Italy
2500 N. Mayfair Rd.,
Wauwatosa, WI 53226
maggianos.com

Mix it Up
Cooking Classes ($$$) 🧁
Union Grove, WI
mixitupcookingclasses.com
Mix It Up cooking classes come to you. The business is run by a corporate wellness dietitian, and there is a focus on making healthy foods delicious and fun for kids. You'll make healthy snacks such as zucchini fries, veggie wraps, green smoothies, and treats like ice cream and peanut butter.

Superior Equipment & Supply Cooking Classes ($$$) 🧁
4550 South Brust Ave.,
Milwaukee, WI 53235
superiorequipmentsupplies. com
Superior Equipment and Supply offers cooking classes and camps for kids and teens throughout the year. Young chefs will be introduced to cooking vocabulary & techniques, tools and utensils, basics of etiquette, nutrition, safety, math and new foods.

Sur la Table ($$$)

Bayshore Town Center
5800 N. Bayshore Dr.,
Glendale, WI 53217
surlatable.com
Check their schedule online
or stop into their store for the
latest information about kids'
cooking classes and camps
at Sur La Table.

The Secret Oven ($$$)

7821 N. Fairchild Rd.,
Fox Point, WI 53217
thesecretoven.com
In small, hands-on classes, kids
ages seven and up learn basic
skills needed to make nutritious
foods. The Secret Oven uses
all natural, organic, and local
ingredients whenever possible
and only natural food colorings
derived from plants and
vegetables. For birthday parties,
choose from themes such as
Cupcake Wars, Pizza Party,
and more. You can also order a
custom birthday cake.

William Sonoma Junior Chef's Cooking Classes (*)

Mayfair Mall
2500 N. Mayfair Rd.,
Wauwatosa, WI 53226
mayfairmall.com/events
Head to William Sonoma at
Mayfair Mall for occasional Junior
Chef's Cooking Classes with
themes such as smoothie-making
and homemade ice cream. Check
Mayfair Mall's calendar of events
for dates and times.

Dance

Top pick:
Danceworks ($$$) 🧁 🕯️
1661 N. Water St.,
Milwaukee, WI 53202
(414) 277-8480
danceworksmke.org

Danceworks is a non-profit, community based dance center for all ages that offers studio classes, camps and workshops. Their programs take place at the downtown Water Street studio, with additional satellite classes held at the Harry & Rose Samson Family Jewish Community Center (JCC) in Whitefish Bay and the Milwaukee Youth Arts Center (MYAC) downtown.

Danceworks also participates in community engagement, including running the Mad Hot Ballroom program which teaches salsa, tango, and swing dance steps to students in dozens of participating schools. These young people then perform their moves on the floor of the BMO Harris Bradley Center.

Top Pick: Milwaukee Ballet School & Academy ($$$)
Locations in Milwaukee, Fox Point, Brookfield, & Hartford
(414) 228-8128
milwaukeeballetschool.org
Study classical ballet with professionals and live piano accompaniment. Enjoy performance opportunities with Milwaukee Ballet Company, student performances, and ticket discounts to Milwaukee Ballet Company performances. Perform alongside the professional dancers in Milwaukee Ballet Company productions like The Nutcracker, and in full length productions designed for all students at no additional charge. Milwaukee Ballet School also offers unique classes for boys. They have locations in Milwaukee, Brookfield, and Fox Point.

Academy of Dance Arts ($$$)
9036 N. 51st St.,
Brown Deer, WI 53223
(414) 354-8020
adaofwisc.com
Academy of Dance Arts offers classes in Ballet, Jazz, Tap, Hip-Hop, Pointe, Modern, and Irish. It is a performance-based school

and provides opportunities for the dancers to perform at a variety of different venues. Students at ADA have performed at Milwaukee Wave Games, Summerfest, Festal Italiana, Lakefront Festival of the Arts, July 4th Celebrations, State Fair, Nursing Homes, Disney World, and the Macy's Thanksgiving Day Parade.

Academy of Performing Arts ($$$)

academywi.com

9160 S. Pennsylvania Ave.,
Oak Creek, WI 53154
(414) 768-0101

10001 St. Martins Rd.,
Franklin, WI 53132
(414) 427-1212

APA offers dance classes starting at age two in state of the art facilities. Both locations also offer private music lessons as well as group GLEE classes for grades two through five. There are optional performance opportunities for the dance and music classes. The Oak Creek location also offers an Academic and Fine Arts Preschool for ages three to four. You can try one class for free by simply giving them a call or heading to their website to register.

They also host several free events throughout the year that are open to the public, including Trunk or Treat (safe Halloween trick or treating), a community Christmas party, and a community Easter Egg Hunt. They also put on dance events

throughout the year including dance camps and Try it Free week.

Anita's Dance Center ($$$)

S63 W13700 Janesville Rd., Muskego, WI 53150
(414) 427-8600
anitasdancecenter.com

Aspire Dance and Music ($$$)

2327 Silvernail Rd., Pewaukee, WI 53072
(262) 349-4088
aspiredancemusic.com

Beginners at every age are welcome, and students can also take music lessons at the same location. Parents & families can view all classes in session through one-way glass observation windows. Aspire offers two performance opportunities for all of their students each year, and their competitive Company Dancers perform at the Bucks Game, Summerfest, and State Fair each year.

Bella Via Dance Studio ($$$)

1220 W. Ranchito Ln., Unit C, Mequon, WI 53092
(262) 236-9298
bellaviadancestudio.com

Brookfield Center for the Arts ($$$) 🧁🔥
2945 N. Brookfield Rd.,
Brookfield, WI 53045
(262) 923-7107
brookfieldcenterforthearts.com

Cashel Dennehy School of Irish Dance ($$$) 🧁🔥
9205 W Center St.,
Wauwatosa, WI 53222
(414) 773-9133
casheldennehy.org

Dancercise Kids Studio Saturdays ($$$)
www.creativecaterpillarkids.com
Dancercise Kids offers studio classes and dance classes at day care centers. The classes incorporate fitness, muscle education, various styles of dance (ballet, jazz, tap), creative movements, and gymnastics.

Dynamite Dance Studio ($$$) 🧁🔥
Falls Plaza II
N81W14972 Appleton Ave.,
Menomonee Falls, WI 53051
(262) 251-4564
dynamitedancestudio.com

Liberty Dance Center ($$$) 🧁🔥
404 Travis Ln., # 37,
Waukesha, WI 53189
(262) 349-9698
libertydancecenter.com
Liberty Dance Center is a family-centered dance studio that performs for veterans, senior citizens, and charitable recitals. The studio also hosts Darby's

Dancers, a free dance education program for children with special needs. There is a competitive team, but there is also a strong focus on life skills.

Miss Becky's Dance Studio ($$$) 🧁🔥
5158 S. 108th St.,
Hales Corners, WI 53130
(414) 425-5715
dancewithmissbecky.com

Nancy Dianne Studio of Dance ($$$)
W178 N9303 Water Tower Pl.,
Menomonee Falls, WI 53051
(262) 251-3940
nancydiannestudioofdance.com

Prime Technique Dance Academy ($$$)
2836 S. Chase Ave.,
Milwaukee, WI 53207
primetechniquedanceacademy.info
Prime Technique Dance Academy offers ballet and tap classes for toddlers through adults. Located in Bay View, the facility features hardwood flooring, mirrors, ballet barres at child-accessible heights, dance mirrors, and a closed circuit observation television which allows parents to view class from the waiting area.

Showcase Dance Studio ($$$)
3380 E. Layton Ave.,
Cudahy, WI 53110
(414) 803-8228
showcasedance.org

Starz Dance Academy ($$$)🧁🔥⛺

S83 W18430 Saturn Dr.,
Muskego, WI 53150
(262) 682-4419
starzdanceacademywi.com
Starz Dance Academy offers studio classes, a competitive pom program, dance fitness classes, birthday parties & more.

Trinity Academy of Irish Dance ($$$)⛺

Locations in Milwaukee, Grafton, Brookfield, Muskego
(877) 326-2328
trinityirishdance.com

Young Dance Academy ($$$)⛺

181 West Marquette Ave.,
Oak Creek, WI 53154
(414) 768-9876
youngdance.biz
Young Dance Academy has been in business since 1983 and trains dancers in ballet, jazz, tap, hip hop, lyrical/contemporary, musical theater and more. Young Dance Academy dancers have competed regionally and nationally in a competitive program since 1991.

Gymnastics & Tumbling

Many of the following locations not only offer formal gymnastics classes, but also open gym times for kids and families to burn some energy on their gymnastics equipments, mats, foam pits, and trampolines. Check their website for the most up-to-date information.

Infinite Gymnastics ($ / $$$)🧁🔥⛺

8989 N. 55th St.,
Brown Deer, WI 53223
infinitegymnastics.com

LaFleur's Gymnastics Academy ($ / $$$)🧁⛺

W189n10991 Klienmann Dr.,
Germantown, WI 53022
lafleursgym.com

Milwaukee Turners Gymnastics🧁

1034 North 4th St.,
Milwaukee, WI 53203
milwaukeeturners.org

North Shore Academy of Gymnastics🧁

W59 N270 Cardinal Ave.,
Cedarburg, WI 53012
northshoregymnastics-wi.com

Salto 🧁
21950 Doral Road,
Brookfield, WI 53186
salto-gym.com

Swiss Turners 🧁
2214 S. 116th St.,
Milwaukee, WI 53227
swissturnersgymnastics.com

Wildcard Gymnastics 🏠🔥
3545 N. 127th St.,
Brookfield, WI 53005
wildcard-gymnastics.com

Flips4All Gymnastics 🏠🔥
4650 N. Port Washington Rd.,
Glendale, WI 53212
flips4all.net

Language & Culture

Alliance Francaise de Milwaukee ($$$) 🔥
Shorewood, WI
afmilwaukee.org
This is the perfect place for mini francophiles to learn about France, French culture, and take language classes.

Kulturvereinigung Deutsche Schule Milwaukee ($$$)
germanschoolmilwaukee.com
This German language school offers classes starting at age three.

Milwaukee Irish Fest Summer School (ages 7 - 12) ($$$)
CelticMKE Center in Wauwatosa
irishfestsummerschool.com
Kids will learn about Irish music, cooking, crafts, storytelling and more.

North American Chinese School ($$$)
northamericanchineseschool.com
Take Chinese language classes and learn more about Chinese culture at one of the North American Chinese School's three locations. They offer both traditional and non-traditional courses for students of all ages.

Music

Milwaukee is home to a vibrant local music scene for kids and families. Read on to learn about organizations that provide top-notch music lessons, live entertainment, and enriching experiences.

414 Live (*)
88.9 Performance Space 220 E. Pittsburgh Ave., Milwaukee, WI 53204
radiomilwaukee.com
To introduce your kids to live, local music, head to one of 88.9's 414 Live concerts, held every Thursday at 5:30 p.m. It's free and open to the public, and you can get your beer, wine, or coffee at Stone Creek Coffee.

Brookfield Center for the Arts ($$$) 🔥
2945 N. Brookfield Rd., Brookfield, WI 53045
brookfieldcenterforthearts.com
The Brookfield Center for the Arts offers music classes for ages 0 and up, as well as dance and theater classes.

Festival City Symphony (* / $)
festivalcitysymphony.org
Festival City Symphony offers Pajama Jamborees for kids, which are free and casual family-friendly classical concerts for all ages, held at the Marcus Center for the Performing Arts. They also offer Symphony Sundays, affordable symphony performances that are specifically open to families and held in the Pabst Theater.

Fox & Branch (*)
foxandbranch.com
Fox and Branch concerts are lively and fun for the whole family. The duo performs an eclectic mix of folk music that is catchy and entertaining for both kids and adults. The audience is encouraged to sing along and participate, and the concerts have a light-hearted vibe.

They perform free concerts at Anodyne Coffee in Walker's Point on select dates throughout the year, and you'll also find them in schools and libraries.

Gospel Brunch & MSO Mondays (*)

Various Colectivo locations
colectivocoffee.com

Uplift your spirit by attending Gospel Brunch, hosted at Colectivo on Prospect in the Back Room on select Sundays. The free concerts feature local gospel groups in quartet tradition. You can also head to various Colectivo locations on select Monday evenings for Milwaukee Symphony Mondays. These free concerts feature members of the Milwaukee Symphony Orchestra. Check the Colectivo website for the latest Gospel Brunch and MSO Mondays schedule.

Jazz Gallery Center for the Arts (*)

Milwaukee, WI
riverwestart.org

Head to this unique community space in Riverwest for scratch sessions, open jazz jams, and more. During the Scratch Sessions, free turntable lessons are offered to young people older than 12. This gallery is on the cutting edge of the local music scene, fostering the creative energy of Milwaukee's young musicians.

Milwaukee Youth Symphony Orchestra ($$$)

325 W. Walnut St.,
Milwaukee, WI 53212
myso.org

Milwaukee Youth Symphony Orchestra (MYSO) is one of the most successful and respected youth orchestra programs in the nation, regularly recognized for its artistic excellence. MYSO offers more than 25 ensemble options, ranging from symphony and string orchestras, to jazz and steel pan bands, all providing high quality musical experiences to students at various skill levels. MYSO offers music camps such as Jazz Guitar Ensemble and Calypso Steel Band Camp.

Music for Aardvarks Milwaukee

milwaukeeaardvarks.com

Music for Aardvarks provides hands-on and interactive music classes for young kids ages 6 months to five years old and their parents at various locations throughout the northern suburbs. The classes are intimate and lively and last 45 minutes. Class activities include live music, sing-a-longs, free dances, and instrument jams with shakers, drums, tambourines, and more. Aardvarks teachers Ms. Jen and Ms. Rachel created the dynamic "kindie rock" band Ms. Jen and the Jellyfish. They perform at area festivals and also do private parties and events.

Music Together ($$$)

musictogether.com

Music Together is an internationally recognized early childhood music and movement program for children from birth through age seven and the grownups who care for them. The classes are hands on and interactive, and come with a CD to listen to at home.

Wisconsin Conservatory of Music ($$$)

1584 N. Prospect Ave.,
Milwaukee, WI 53202
wcmusic.org

The Conservatory offers music lessons and camps for all ages, as well as concerts, recitals, and other special events. Choose from a wide variety of themed music camps with a full-day format to fit your schedule.

School of Rock ($$$)

4050 N. Oakland Ave.,
Shorewood, WI 53211
shorewood.schoolofrock.com

School of Rock offers guitar, drum, bass, piano and keyboard, and singing lessons. The lessons are performance based and use classic and popular songs that kids will love. They're designed to instill a life-long passion for music.

Sharon Lynne Wilson Center for Arts ($$$)

19805 W. Capitol Dr.,
Brookfield, WI 53045
wilson-center.com

This arts center offers youth and family music classes starting at age one. Their music classes are offered through the Wisconsin Conservatory of Music.

Running

Girls on the Run ($$$)

girlsontherunsoutheasternwi.org

Girls on the Run is a program for girls in 3rd-5th grade that helps girls foster self-confidence, healthy friendships, compassion, physical fitness, and community-mindedness, all through running and a team-organized community project. Each season culminates with a Girls on the Run 5K event, a celebratory, non-competitive event that helps participants practice goal-setting and gives them a sense of accomplishment. There is also a similar middle school program tailored for girls in 6th-8th grade.

Soccer

Lil' Kickers ($$$) 🧁 🔥
In-Bounds Training Center
2920 W. Vera Rd.,
Glendale, WI 53209
inboundstraining.com

Lil' Kickers soccer classes are held at the In-Bounds Training Center in Glendale, a modern, spacious indoor facility complete with wi-fi, a cafe serving local coffee, slushies, and snacks, plus lots of seating for parents who want to watch their kids.

Midwest Orthopedic Sports Complex ($$$)
19485 Lisbon Rd.,
Brookfield, WI 53045
brookfieldindoor.com
This 80,000 square foot facility has three huge fields equipped with a state of the art playing surface. This sports complex is home to a youth soccer program, and also offers youth rugby and flag football.

Milwaukee Kickers ($$$) 🧁 🔥
Uihlein Soccer Park
7101 W. Good Hope Rd.,
Milwaukee, WI 53223
mksc.org
Young campers will participate in games, activities and scrimmages designed to teach the basics of soccer. First time players are welcome, while older kids will maximize their level of skill through training techniques and games.

Milwaukee Wave Summer Camps ($$$) 🔥
milwaukeewave.com
Youth Soccer Academy Camps start at age four and are led by former professional soccer players and licensed coaches. Campers learn the fundamentals of the sport including passing, shooting, dribbling and receiving. Kids will participate in scrimmages and other games. The camp's coaching staff is trained and certified by the Milwaukee Kickers.

Sewing

MKE Fashion Incubator ($$$) 🏠 🔥
1422 N. 4th St.,
Milwaukee, WI 53212
mkefashionincubator.com
MKE Fashion Incubator is a collaborative space where kids and adults can take sewing, design, and pattern classes or participate in family fun workshops. They host business meet-ups, camps, and birthday parties, as well.

Swimming Lessons

Top pick:
Goldfish Swim School ($$$) 🏠
12565 W. Feerick St.,
Brookfield, WI 53005
(262) 207-2800
goldfishswimschool.com/
brookfield
Goldfish Swim School provides swim instruction to children ages four months to 12 years-old in a tropical themed, 9.000 square foot facility. Their classes are small, with a maximum four to one student to teacher ratio, and their pools are always warm at 90 degrees. Plus, you can watch your swimmer from an air conditioned viewing gallery.

Splash! ($$$) 🏠
10636 N. Commerce St.,
Mequon, WI 53092
(262) 512-SWIM (7946)
splashmequon.com
Learn to swim or prepare for competitive swim teams at Splash! in Mequon. The pool is kept at 90 degrees, and classes starts at six months old.

Swimtastic Swim School ($$$) 🏠
Locations in Franklin and Waukesha
swimtastic.com

Yoga

Not every yoga studio offers yoga classes for kids, but the ones in this chapter most certainly do. Call ahead or check their websites for the most updated classes and schedules.

OmTown Yogis (*)

omtownyogis.org

OmTown Yogis is a yoga community in Milwaukee that provides monthly yoga classes at the Art Museum and in Milwaukee parks during warm weather. Their Yoga at the Library series offers occasional classes especially for kids and families. Check their website for dates and times.

Copper Tree Yoga Studio ($$)

Hartford, WI
studio.hopecorefitness.com

Empower Yoga Milwaukee ($)

Whitefish Bay, WI
empoweryogamilwaukee.com

Healium Hot Yoga ($$)

Milwaukee, WI
healiumhotyoga.com
(Kids classes not heated)

Inner Light Yoga Studios ($$)

Wauwatosa, WI
innerlightyogastudios.com

The Womb Room

Milwaukee, WI
facebook.com/
thewombroommke

Resources
Pregnancy & Breastfeeding

Authentic Birth Center & Wellness Collective
530 N. 108th Pl.,
Wauwatosa, WI 53226
(414) 231-9640
authenticbirthcenter.com
Authentic Birth Center & Wellness Collective offers midwifery care, family support services, health care, and education in the Milwaukee area. Check their website for fun classes like mom and baby music, pre and post-natal yoga, and baby-wearing workshops.

Columbia Center
13125 N. Port Washington Rd., Mequon, WI 53097
(262) 243-7408
thebirthhospital.org
Columbia Center is a specialty hospital dedicated exclusively to birth. It offers a modern, spa-like environment that conceals the latest medical technology. They also offer a doula program.

Mothering the Mother
1588 S. 81st St.,
West Allis, WI 53214
(414) 446-7107
motheringthemotherinc.org
Mothering the Mother is a non-profit organization dedicated to improving pregnancy, childbirth, and motherhood experiences for all women by providing a lending library, prenatal care coordination services, educational classes, birth doulas for continuous labor support, lactation support for improved breastfeeding success, postpartum doulas to help with the new transitions the family is experiencing, support groups, and mentors.

La Leche League of Wisconsin
llli.org
La Leche League of Wisconsin is a branch of an international, nonprofit, nonsectarian organization dedicated to providing education, information, support, and encouragement to women who want to breastfeed. All women interested in breastfeeding are welcome

to attend the monthly group meetings or call a leader for breastfeeding help.

Columbia St. Mary's
2301 N. Lake Dr.,
Milwaukee, WI 53211
(414) 291-1000
columbia-stmarys.org
Columbia St. Mary's offers breastfeeding classes and a wide range of other pre and post-natal classes.

Bay View Family Wellness
2455 S. Howell Ave.,
Milwaukee, WI 53207
(414) 628-7659
bayviewfamilywellness.com
Bay View Family Wellness offers private lactation services. Office visits are provided within Well-Rounded Maternity Center in Bay View and Authentic Birth Center in Wauwatosa.

Aurora Health Care
aurorahealthcare.org
Aurora Health Care offers a wide variety of classes and community events, including lactation services, pre-natal yoga, and post-natal yoga.

Nurturing Newborns
(414) 763-5158
nurturingnewborncare.com
Nurturing Newborns offers postpartum doula and newborn care, baby planner and concierge services, child care and nanny consultations, overnight services and night nanny referrals, and sleep consultations.

Milwaukee Babywearers
milwaukeebabywearing.com
Milwaukee Babywearers is a local, volunteer run group that promotes baby-wearing. They provide free classes, forums for discussions, and organized playgroups.

MommyFit Milwaukee
facebook.com/
MommyFitMilwaukee/
MommyFit Milwaukee is a group of moms who exercise together while spending time with their little one. Visit their Facebook page for information and details.

Breastfeeding Stations

If you prefer to nurse in a quiet place, here are some places that offer nursing lounges and pods:

Mamava Lactation Stations at Mitchell International Airport, Miller Park, and the Milwaukee County Zoo.

Betty Brinn Children's Museum:
Nursing nook in the baby area in Pocket Park.

Buy Buy Baby (Brookfield):
Nursing and changing station to the left of the entrance.

Bayshore Town Center:
Nursing room near the restrooms off of the food court.

Mayfair Mall:
Located in the food court family restroom

Community Centers

Bay View Community Center
1320 E. Oklahoma Ave.,
Milwaukee, WI 53207
(414) 482-1000
bayviewcenter.org

Boys and Girls Club of Greater Milwaukee
1558 N. 6th St.,
Milwaukee, WI 53212
(414) 267-8100
boysgirlsclubs.org

COA Youth and Family Services
2320 W. Burleigh St.,
Milwaukee, WI 53206
(414) 449-1757
coa-yfc.org
COA's Harry and Rose Samson Family Resource Center (FRC) provides fun, interactive activities for families with kids from birth to six. The center offers drop-in programming that includes free play, art projects, reading, songs, snacks and more. Parents can also make connections with other families and local resources to support them.

Jewish Community Center
6255 N. Santa Monica Blvd.,
Whitefish Bay, WI 53217
(414) 967-8200
jccmilwaukee.org

Kosciuszko Community Center
2201 S. 7th St.,
Milwaukee, WI 53215
(414) 645-4624
county.milwaukee.gov

St. Ann Center for Intergenerational Care
2801 E. Morgan Ave.,
Milwaukee, WI 53207
(414) 977-5000
stanncenter.org

United Community Center
1028 S. 9th St.,
Milwaukee, WI 53204
(414) 384-3100
unitedcc.org

YMCA of Metropolitan Milwaukee
ymcamke.org

Recreation Departments

Milwaukee Recreation
Department
(414) 475-8180
milwaukeerecreation.net

Brookfield Parks,
Recreation & Forestry
Department
(262) 796-6675
ci.brookfield.wi.us

Brown Deer Parks
and Recreation
(414) 371-3070
browndeerwi.org

Cedarburg Recreation
Department
(262) 375-7600
ci.cedarburg.wi.us

Cudahy Parks
and Recreation
cudahy-wi.gov

Greendale Parks
and Recreation
(414) 423-2790
gpr.greendale.k12.wi.us

Greenfield Parks
and Recreation
(414) 329-5370
ci.greenfield.wi.us

Franklin Community
Education and Recreation
Department
(414) 423-4646
franklin.k12.wi.us

Hales Corners Recreation
Department
(414) 529-6161
halescorners.org

Menomonee Falls
Community Education
and Recreation
(262) 255-8460
fallrec.org

Mequon-Thiensville
Recreation Department
(262) 238-8500
mtsd.k12.wi.us

Town of Mukwonago Parks
and Recreation
(262) 363-7077
townofmukwonago.us

Muskego Parks
and Recreation
(262) 679-4108
cityofmuskego.org

New Berlin Recreation
Department
(262) 797-2443
newberlin.org

Nicolet Recreation Department
(414) 351-7566
nicolet.k12.wi.us

Shorewood Recreation & Community Services
(414) 963-6913 ext. 4
shorewood.k12.wi.us

St. Francis Recreation
(414) 747-3900
stfrancisschools.org/schools/recreation

Wauwatosa Recreation Department
(414) 773-2900
register.tosarec.com

West Allis-West Milwaukee Recreation Department
(414) 604-4900
wawmrec.com

Whitefish Bay Recreation and Community Education Department
(414) 963-3947
wfbschools.com

Special Needs

If you or a friend or family member has a child with special needs, the organizations in this resource guide might help to enrich your lives and navigate the challenges you may be facing.

Broadscope Disability Services
6102 W. Layton Ave., Greenfield, WI 53220
(414) 329-4500
broadscope.org
Broadscope provides respite options for caregivers, with locations in Milwaukee and Waukesha.

Curative Care Network
curative.org
Curative Care provides high quality services to children, adults and seniors with disabilities or limiting conditions in southeast Wisconsin.

Down Syndrome Association of Wisconsin

11709 W. Cleveland Ave.
Suite 2,
West Allis, WI 53227
(414) 327-3729
dsaw.org
Easter Seals Southeast Wisconsin provides services to ensure that all people with disabilities or special needs and their families have opportunities to live, learn, work and play in their communities.

Donna Lexa Art Centers

donnalexa.org

247 Wisconsin Ave.,
Waukesha, WI 53186
262-521-2292

1345 S. 47th St.,
West Milwaukee, WI 53214
262-888-2861
At Donna Lexa Community Art Centers, they promote and celebrate the following core values: Creativity, Curiosity, Friendship, Respect, Growth and Success.

The Donna Lexa Art Centers currently serve adults and teens with cognitive and physical disabilities, as well as individuals with mental health concerns. In addition, they provide art classes for senior citizens dealing with the challenges of aging.

Easter Seals Southeast Wisconsin

2222 S. 114th St.,
West Allis, WI 53227
(414) 449-4444
easterseals.com
Easter Seals Southeast Wisconsin provides services to ensure that all people with disabilities or special needs and their families have opportunities to live, learn, work and play in their communities.

First Stage Next Steps

325 W. Walnut St.,
Milwaukee, WI 53212
(414) 267-2929
firststage.org
Next Steps classes are designed to help students with autism take their next steps as an artist and a person, allowing them the opportunity to learn social skills among their peers while participating in theatrical and musical activities.

First Stage also provides sensory friendly performances of their shows for children with autism that feature smaller audience sizes, reduced loud noises and flashing lights, designated quiet areas, and even noise-cancelling headphones.

194

Gigi's Playhouse
8685 N. Port Washington Rd.,
Fox Point, WI 53217
(414) 797-0522
gigisplayhouse.org
This Down Syndrome
Achievement Center leads
campaigns and educational
programs, and offers free
therapeutic and educational
programming to individuals
with Down Syndrome and
their families.

Independence First
540 S. 1st St.,
Milwaukee, WI 53204
(414) 291-7520
independencefirst.org
Independence First helps kids
and adults with disabilities build
skills for self-sufficiency.

Liberty Dance Center ($$$)
404 Travis Ln., #37,
Waukesha, WI 53189
(262) 349-9698
libertydancecenter.com
The studio hosts Darby's
Dancers, a free dance education
program for children with
special needs.

Life Navigators
7203 W. Center St.,
Wauwatosa, WI 53210
(414) 774-6255
lifenavigators.org
Life Navigators provides
opportunities and services for
children with intellectual and
developmental disabilities.

Milwaukee Ballet Tour de Force
milwaukeeballet.org
In French, "tour de force" can
be translated as a "vital step."
Milwaukee Ballet and Children's
Hospital of Wisconsin offer
children with disabilities a
beginning ballet class and the
chance to use their muscles
and minds in new ways. At the
close of the five-week sessions,
the children enjoy a Milwaukee
Ballet performance.

Milwaukee Center for Independence 🔥
2020 W. Wells St.,
Milwaukee, WI 53233
(414) 937-2020
mcfi.net
MCFI offers services to help
children with disabilities,
profound medical issues, and
special needs reach their full
potential.

Playgrounds -
Check out the playgrounds
chapter for information
about inclusive
playgrounds around
Milwaukee. (Pg. 127)

Miracle League of Wisconsin

Werner Family
Foundation Field
9050 N. Swan Rd.,
Milwaukee, WI 53224
miracleleaguemilwaukee.org
The Miracle League allows
all children to play organized
baseball, regardless of ability.
Kids with special-needs dress
in uniforms, make plays in the
field and round the bases, just
like their peers in standard little
leagues. Miracle League baseball
is played on a custom-designed
field featuring a cushioned,
rubberized, completely flat
surface to prevent injuries
and allow access for the
visually impaired and those in
wheelchairs. All areas of the
field, including the dugouts
and restrooms, are universally
accessible.

Office for Persons with Disabilities

901 N. 9th St., Room 307-B,
Milwaukee, WI 53233
(414) 278-3932
county.milwaukee.gov/OPD
The OPD provides services that
make County programs, services,
and facilities accessible to people
with disabilities.

Penfield Children's Center

833 N. 26th St.,
Milwaukee, WI 53233
(414) 344-7676
penfieldbuildingblocks.org
Penfield Children's Center helps
children reach age appropriate
milestones and enter school
ready to learn. Their speech
pathologists, physical and
occupational therapists, special
education teachers, nurses, social
workers, and early education
professionals help children
overcome developmental
challenges.

St. Ann Center for Intergenerational Care

stanncenter.org

Stein Campus:
(414) 977-5000
2801 E. Morgan Ave.,
Milwaukee, WI 53207

Bucyrus Campus:
(414) 210-2450
2450 W. North Ave.,
Milwaukee, WI 53205
St. Ann Center is an adult and
child day care center open 6am
to 6pmMonday through Friday.
The center cares for children,
plus adults (those over 17) with
disabilities and the frail elderly
as well as being a support for
their families and caregivers. St.
Ann Center provides community-
based care that meets each
individuals needs and helps
them experience the joys of
life through art, music and
interactions with people all
ages and abilities.

The Richardson School

richardsonschool.com

6753 W. Rogers St.,
West Allis, WI 53219

175 S. Barker Rd.,
Brookfield, WI 53045

The Richardson School is a therapeutic day school located in your community that specializes in working with children, adolescents and young adults who have diagnoses of developmental/neurological disabilities, and behavioral and emotional issues.

United Cerebral Palsy of Southeast Wisconsin

6102 W. Layton Ave.,
Greenfield, WI 53220
(414) 329-4500
ucpsew.org

United Cerebral Palsy of Southeastern Wisconsin promotes the independence and productivity of people with cerebral palsy and other disabilities.

Vision Forward

912 North Hawley Rd.,
Milwaukee, WI 53213
(414) 615-0100
vision-forward.org

Vision Forward empowers, educates and enhances the lives of individuals with vision loss.

Wisconsin First Step

mch-hotlines.org

Wisconsin First Step assists parents in finding resources for their children with special needs.

Wisconsin Upside Down

155 East Capitol Drive,
Suite 1,
Hartland, WI 53029
(262) 443-8690
wiusd.org

Wisconsin Upside Down is dedicated to enhancing the lives of individuals with Down syndrome. The mission of Wisconsin Upside Down is to offer Down syndrome Advocacy, Education, Awareness and Support to families of individuals with Down syndrome and the community.

Zachariah's Acres

N74W35911 Servants' Way,
Oconomowoc, WI 53066
(262) 825-3737
zachariahsacres.org

Zachariah's Acres offers 48 pristine acres where kids with special needs and their families can enjoy nature and experience the outdoors and learn about agriculture and nature.

CPSIA information can be obtained
at www.ICGtesting.com
Printed in the USA
JSHW020052160120
3579JS00002BA/9

9 781948 365871